ACCOLADES FOR

ENLIGHTENED BOTTOM LINE

"Jenna Nicholas masterfully explores how spirituality can inform and elevate our financial and business choices. Her book is an invitation to rethink success—not just as profit, but also as purpose and positive impact."

—**Rainn Wilson,** actor, philanthropist and *New York Times* bestselling author of *Soul Boom*

"Jenna Nicholas's *Enlightened Bottom Line* provides vital insights for anyone seeking to align values with business goals. Her unique perspective and beautiful writing style make this a valuable resource for conscious investors and leaders alike."

—**Sarah Soule,** dean, Stanford Graduate School of Business

"Jenna Nicholas invites us all to imagine a future where business decisions are guided by empathy and meaning. Her book is practical, hopeful, and accessible to anyone who wants to make the world better."

—**Lynne Twist,** bestselling author of *The Soul of Money*

"At a time when political, financial, and social systems are all under stress, Jenna Nicholas's voice and principles create an inspiring model to break through the clutter and tools to leverage the financial system to create change."

—**Rachel Robasciotti,** cofounder of Adasina Social Capital

ENLIGHTENED BOTTOM LINE

Exploring the Intersection of Spirituality, Business, and Investing

JENNA NICHOLAS

www.amplifypublishinggroup.com

Enlightened Bottom Line: Exploring the Intersection of Spirituality, Business, and Investing

For more information, please contact:
Amplify Publishing, an imprint of Amplify Publishing Group
620 Herndon Parkway, Suite 220
Herndon, VA 20170
info@amplifypublishing.com

Library of Congress Control Number: 2025926852

CPSIA Code: PRV0126A

ISBN-13: 979-8-90026-015-0

Printed in the United States

To my mum, my grandmother, and all the ancestors who continue to guide us to walk the spiritual path with practical feet

CONTENTS

FOREWORD

No one disputes that we are living in times of rapid change and profound uncertainty. The debate has more to do with what that means, both for humanity in general and for business leaders, founders, and investors. Many see this period of accelerating technology and change as even more reason to lean into cutthroat competition, division, and exploitation, all in the name of maximizing profit.

Others (rightly) see that the need to connect deeper values to how we conduct business and steward our resources has never been more pressing. Jenna Nicholas is one such leader, entrepreneur, and investor. Her decades of work at the crossroads of finance, entrepreneurship, and spiritual engagement intersected with my own more than ten years ago, when Jenna and I collaborated to foster values-driven investing and business practices in China and around the world. The results were not just healthy, sustainable economic growth for the companies and funds that we invested in but also lasting, positive impact. This proves that our markets and economies are not just mechanisms for profit but also meaningful expressions of our shared humanity and a potential force for collective healing.

Jenna is part of a generation of leaders who are rising to push the movement of social impact investing forward at the intersection of spiritual consciousness and business. I can attest to the power of this approach, in terms of both impact and growth. I built Calvert Funds, a pioneer in the socially responsible investing industry, in 1976 when this concept was nascent in the United States and around the world. It now has $45 billion in assets under management. Given the challenges in the world right now, we need a generation of leaders to rise to meet these challenges and expand the work started by Calvert and others in the movement. I am so proud that Jenna has chosen to take up this mantle and continue this important work.

Jenna approaches investing and business with rare integrity, thoughtfulness, and vision. Her commitment to weaving spirituality into decision-making demonstrates how business, at its best, can be an instrument for personal growth and global transformation. I have observed firsthand her capacity to listen deeply, act boldly, and inspire others to search for purpose beyond merely the bottom line. Her passion, clarity, and deep commitment serve to catalyze capital, policies, and people to meet the challenges of climate change and other areas of impact.

This book arrives at an essential moment. With political, environmental, and economic turbulence rippling across the globe, Jenna's exploration of spirituality in the realms of investing and business offers a map toward greater connectedness and conscious action. She invites us to pause, to reflect, and to reconsider the motives and impacts behind our financial choices. In doing so, she empowers us to ask not just what we can achieve but also what (and whom) we truly serve, how we serve, and why.

The insights and stories shared here represent a call to action not only to reimagine what business can be but also to discover how integrating spirit within commerce can uplift communities, nurture the planet, and respond compassionately to the world's urgent challenges. Jenna's work calls us to move beyond division and scarcity and toward wholeness and abundance. This has been exemplified through Jenna's investing efforts as well as through her convening and facilitation work with Impact Experience, where I serve on the board.

I am grateful for Jenna's leadership, and I celebrate the wisdom woven throughout these pages. May they inspire in you, as they have in me, a renewed sense of possibility and purpose.

—**Wayne Silby**, founding chair, Calvert Funds

INTRODUCTION

Embedding Spirituality in Business and Investing

Have you ever wondered what your tombstone might say? If you had to—honestly—reduce the sum of your impact on this world to a single line, chiseled in stone, what words come to mind?

That is exactly what my colleague Wayne Silby was asked to do at a Buddhist retreat back in the 1970s, soon after he founded Calvert Funds. At the time, he had been hustling to compete in a high-paced investment market, and his reflections yielded a nightmarish vision of his earthly "achievements":

Here lies Wayne, who made 2 percent more than the next guy.

Needless to say, this was not the legacy Silby wanted to leave. Upon his return to the office, he led his entire management team to reflect on their overall purpose in building an organization. Silby wanted to make a positive impact in addition to driving financial success, so the company laid out its mission to meet the needs of return-seeking investors today while also focusing on the long-term needs of our planet and society.

Calvert has since become a pioneer in the area of socially responsible investing, with approximately $45 billion in assets now under management. Some examples of Calvert's impact include investing in health technology companies that innovate diagnostics for early detection of major diseases and investing in education technology companies that democratize education. Overall, the firm's work has played a significant role in shaping the trillion-dollar impact investing industry . . . and it all started with a meditation on life, death, and legacy.

This book is an invitation for similar reflection and impact—a call to journey together where the sacred and the practical meet. Where the choices we make about money become acts of service to one another, the earth, and those yet to come. Here we explore how money, when tended with care, can become a living force for healing, regeneration, and connection.

Again and again, business leaders and investors have shared with me their stories—moments that cracked them open, that unsettled and remade them. Often their voices would drop and their eyes would search for reassurance as they confessed, "I don't really feel like I can talk about this, but . . ."

They next speak of dark nights of the soul, of wrestling with doubt and emerging with new clarity that reshapes not only their lives but also the very organizations they lead, found, and invest in. They shared moments of personal hardship or loss, combined with pressure to make business or financial decisions that did not align with their values. Many of these courageous individuals chose to take a chance on their higher natures and lean into those values, prioritizing people and our planet over mere profits alone. And they managed to do all of that while also steering their organizations toward greater success.

These stories, when honored and integrated, become the roots from which purpose-driven businesses and investments grow—ventures that nourish not just balance sheets but also the balance among business, communities, and the land itself.

I wrote this book to honor these stories, to create space for a conscious way of leading in business and investing. By bringing these conversations into the light, I hope to kindle a wider recognition: that spirituality, far from being separate from our financial lives, can transform the very way we allocate capital, shifting us from hierarchies and status to service, ethics, and kinship. *What if the way we spend and invest could become a way to heal the world?*

Throughout my career and studies—from London to China to Silicon Valley and through my time at Stanford as an undergraduate and at the Stanford Graduate School of Business—I have walked many paths. I have invested in health care, climate, and education and built coalitions of over 170 foundations, representing more than $50 billion in assets under management to move capital from fossil fuels into impact-driven solutions across asset classes. I co-founded Impact Experience in 2015, an impact-driven organization designed to build bridges between investors and underestimated communities. Again and again, I have witnessed what happens when spirituality gets involved, not as an afterthought but as the very heartbeat of decision-making. Through my work with LightPost Capital, I invest into and acquire companies addressing some of the great challenges of our time. When we measure not only our return on investment but also our return on impact,[1] we create ripples that nourish the world.

This work is certainly not mine alone. I have learned alongside visionary leaders and changemakers who believe, fiercely, that money can become medicine. Together, we have asked, *How can we use our resources to heal, uplift, and meet the urgent challenges of our time? How can we infuse our financial choices with joy, integrity, and freedom?*

The word *spiritual* comes from the Latin *spiritus*, meaning "breath," the animating force of life. This leads me to wonder:

What if we breathed life into our financial systems, infusing them with purpose, consciousness, and the recognition that we are all connected? Just as breath sustains our bodies, a spiritual approach to business and investing can sustain our communities, our ecosystems, and our future. When we remember the root meaning of *spiritual*, we begin to define wealth not only as money but also as the living, breathing well-being of people, relationships, and the planet itself.

To me, a spiritual person is not someone who has arrived but someone who strives—who returns, again and again, to the work of growing, reflecting, and caring for others. I often fall short, but I take heart from the words of Bahá'u'lláh, the nineteenth-century founder of the Bahá'í Faith: "Rest assured and persevere."[2]

In my opinion, the true measure of spirituality is not perfection but the willingness to try, to reflect, and to begin again. In business, this means creating cultures of hope, compassion, and mindful communication—workplaces where creativity and innovation can flourish because people are seen and valued.

Throughout the book, I often write from the perspective of my own faith, the Bahá'í tradition, which teaches that all religions share an underlying unity and that the world's economic challenges require spiritual solutions. The Bahá'í writings offer practical guidance on profit sharing, decision-making, and the roles of management and labor, all rooted in principles that honor our interconnectedness. Business need not be at odds with spirituality; indeed, it can become a powerful force for material and social progress. The Bahá'í vision is nothing less than the recreation of civilization—a world where spiritual principles infuse every institution, from families to global governance.

I will be sharing more examples of thought leaders and changemakers from various industries and spiritual traditions who are trailblazing their way toward creating a more equitable and just world. These leaders integrate spiritual values into the way they use their money in business and investment decisions. They are investors who champion sustainable agriculture, CEOs who partner with local communities, founders who innovate renewable energy sources, and so many more. I have interviewed individuals from all walks of life whose perspectives, insights, and experiences provide a multifaceted exploration of these transformative ideas. A foundational framework revisited throughout the book for integrating spirituality into investing and business is the HEAL model: hope, empathy, abundance, and legacy. Among the people I interviewed, these themes consistently emerged, providing a compass for this book.

An enlightened bottom line asks us to bring our whole selves to work, aligning our personal values with our professional choices. Too often those in finance and business feel they must leave their deepest beliefs at the door, practicing values-driven activities only in their spare time. Many spend their workweeks focused solely on maximizing shareholder value, only to compartmentalize their sense of purpose into a few hours of volunteering on the weekend. But business and impact do not need to be so disconnected. We can align our work and our values so that purpose becomes part of how we create value every day, not just as an afterthought but as a key driver of every decision, every relationship, every investment.

I have seen the power of collaboration—of partners coming together, blending rigorous analysis with deep reflection, asking how spiritual values can inform their strategies, valuations, Gross Domestic Product (GDP), and metrics. This cocreative process uncovers new ways to deploy capital, driving systemic change and contributing to the collective good. In a 2020 essay published by *The Economist*, Canadian Prime Minister Mark Carney[3] stated the following about economic values and human values during the COVID-19 pandemic:

> Value will change in the post-COVID world. On one level, that's obvious: valuations in global financial markets have imploded, with many suffering their sharpest declines in decades. More fundamentally, the traditional drivers of value have been shaken, new ones will gain prominence, and there's a possibility that the gulf between what markets value and what people value will close . . . This crisis could help reverse that relationship, so that public values help shape private values. When pushed, societies have prioritized health first and foremost, and then looked to deal with the economic consequences. In this crisis, we know we need to act as an interdependent community, not independent individuals, so the values of economic dynamism and efficiency have been joined by those of solidarity, fairness, responsibility and compassion.[4]

Reflecting on the intersection between the individual and the collective, Mark Carney agrees with Ralph Waldo Emerson, the American transcendentalist who famously said, "Health is the first wealth." The previous passage demonstrates how, in the wake of a disaster shock, such as COVID-19, we have opportunities to revive the connection between consciousness and economic systems to create transformative change.

Carney is not the first prominent politician to look to integrate human values into economic frameworks. In an address at the University of Kansas in 1968, Robert F. Kennedy once said about the Gross National Product (GNP): ". . . it measures everything, except that which makes life worthwhile."[5] A 2021 editorial by *The Guardian* columnist Larry Elliott put it this way:

> There are not many memorable speeches about gross domestic product, but that may be because the one made by Bobby Kennedy while on the campaign trail in 1968 said it all. As Kennedy pointed out, the production of napalm and nuclear warheads counted towards GDP, but the health of American children and the joy of their play did not.
>
> "It does not include the beauty of our poetry or the strength of our marriages, the intelligence of our public debate or the integrity of our public officials. It measures neither our wit nor our courage, neither our wisdom nor our learning, neither our compassion nor our devotion to our country. It measures everything in short, except that which makes life worthwhile. And it can tell us everything about America except why we are proud that we are Americans."
>
> Those words were true in 1968, and they resonate even more strongly today. Measured by GDP, the US is the world's richest country. Measured by GDP per head, it is one of the richest. Measured in other ways, in life expectancy, for example, the US would be a long way down the international league tables. And as recent events have shown all too clearly, it is not a country at ease with itself.[6]

As a purely quantitative measure, GDP figures tell us nothing about the *quality* of growth. A spiritual approach to business and investing seeks to address this gap by focusing on what truly matters: human dignity, ecological balance, and the collective good. This perspective challenges us to move beyond traditional metrics, embracing a more holistic vision of progress that honors the complexities of our shared humanity.

In the health care industry, where both precision and empathy should be paramount, one great example of integrating spirituality into business is Devoted Health,[7] a company that focuses on Medicare Advantage plans that is valued at over $13 billion. This company exemplifies the transformative impact of integrating personalized care with spiritual principles. Todd Park, cofounder and executive chairman of Devoted Health, emphasizes the power of love as the cornerstone of his organization's mission and the foundation for decision-making. This philosophy not only drives exceptional care for patients but also ensures financial success, proving that compassion and profitability are not mutually exclusive—in fact, they are often deeply interdependent. One defining practice at Devoted Health involves encouraging doctors and care providers to pause before interacting with a patient, close their eyes, and ask themselves this question: *What if this individual were my own beloved family member—a mother, father, or sibling?*

This simple yet profound act shifts the focus away from engaging with patients in a routine way, where patients often feel like numbers, to providing the highest standard of care, one rooted in respect and connection. By fostering a culture of love and personalized attention, Devoted Health exemplifies how spiritual values can elevate health care outcomes and redefine what it means to lead, and grow, with purpose.

The convergence of spirituality, investing, and business can seem paradoxical, as we often view these domains as separate or even conflicting. Among the challenges leaders, founders, and investors face in incorporating sustainability and spirituality into their businesses is the pressure of the shareholder primacy theory from the late 1990s and the related pursuit of short-term shareholder growth (looking only from one quarter/year to the next rather than the longer-term, bigger picture of sustainable growth).

These approaches fall short, even when it comes to (sustainable) material profits. For example, the exploitation of communities and workers, and the degradation of natural resources, often result in costly lawsuits, and shortsighted practices aimed at infinite quarterly growth have led to many business closures.

Let's face it: None of these outcomes would look good on anyone's tombstone. What do you want *your* legacy as a leader, founder, or investor to be? Will you accept this invitation to dig deeper into your own values and spiritual practices—and bring those riches into the world through your business impact?

Spirituality is often associated with detachment from material concerns, while investing and business are deeply rooted in the pursuit of financial gain. However, I believe that the true power lies in embracing this apparent contradiction. In ancient Zen traditions, practitioners sought spiritual enlightenment through meditating on paradoxical riddles, called koans. Similarly, by holding this apparent paradox between the material and the spiritual, leaders can tap into a wellspring of creativity, ethical decision-making, and holistic success. Spiritual principles such as mindfulness, compassion, and interconnectedness can inform executive business practices and investment strategies, leading to more sustainable and socially responsible outcomes that also support business growth.

Conversely, the discipline and strategic thinking cultivated in business and investing can enhance one's spiritual journey, fostering personal growth and a deeper understanding of the world's complexities. Ultimately, those who can navigate this seeming paradox may find themselves uniquely positioned to create value that transcends mere financial metrics, contributing to both personal fulfillment and societal well-being. That is what I mean by the enlightened bottom line.

Join me now in exploring how money can be used as a force of good and how centering spiritual principles in our decision-making around business and investment opportunities can activate the best of humankind in uplifting others and caring for our planet. May this book galvanize you to be an agent of change in providing solutions to our world's current crises and leaving a legacy of impact for future generations to come.

PART 1

CONTEXT SETTING

CHAPTER 1

Creating a Unique Trace

Every choice we make—as an employee or employer, producer or consumer, borrower or lender, benefactor or beneficiary—leaves a trace, and the moral duty to lead a coherent life demands that one's economic decisions be in accordance with lofty ideals, that the purity of one's aims be matched by the purity of one's actions to fulfil those aims.

—THE UNIVERSAL HOUSE OF JUSTICE

As we teeter on the brink of profound global change, spiritual business models can be the incubators for a world where economic decisions honor human dignity and ensure social equity. We do this by meticulously blending spiritual values into everything our organizations do, making sure our actions and choices truly reflect our commitment to principles such as justice, equity, inclusivity, and fairness. By consciously directing our efforts toward inclusivity, we not only foster fairness but also empower underrepresented voices in business and finance. This is vital for the enrichment of our collective future. For example, research by the Corporate Governance Institute found that companies with more diverse boards consistently yield greater long-term profits with less shareholder dissent.[1]

Incorporating more spiritual principles into business and investing can herald a profound shift in how we engage with wealth, resources, and one another—one that recognizes the complexity and interconnectivity of our global community. At the heart of this transformation lies the belief that aligning our investments and business decisions with our values is not only a moral imperative but also a catalyst for change—one that invites us to think more conscientiously and holistically about how we participate in the economic systems shaping our shared future. This process challenges us to overcome biases and assumptions that often distort our judgment and decisions, such as those related to race, class, political, religious, and socioeconomic lines. It necessitates a deep inward reflection on how our organizations live out these spiritual principles and core values as well as an outward look at our interactions and impacts within wider communities.

One component of my work involves creating partnerships between entrepreneurs, investors, artists, and academics, fostering meaningful connections with communities that have been overlooked and underestimated. This forms part of a broader effort to drive systemic change and contribute to impactful, holistic solutions. American Jesuit priest Father Gregory Boyle embodies this approach with his commitment to gang intervention and rehabilitation in Los Angeles, California, through his work with Homeboy Industries. Boyle's stated mission has always been to engage at the margins until the margins disappear. Building bridges across the divides of race, gender, economic background, and religion can craft environments that foster opportunities for genuine connections and mutually enriching collaborations. The process of bridge-building within organizations and communities—creating relationships grounded in deep respect for individuals' varied backgrounds and life experiences—fosters environments that honor the full spectrum of human experience and aspiration while also growing your business.

This idea encourages us to see ourselves as part of a larger interconnected web, understanding that the well-being and success of one entity is inherently and inextricably interdependent on others. It is a perspective that shifts our definition of success from individual victories to collective triumphs, promoting a win-win approach over a zero-sum game.

After investing in socially responsible businesses and funds, I observed a disconnect between investors and the communities in which they were investing. It was this gap that inspired me to cofound Impact Experience.[2] My aim for Impact Experience is to bridge the gap between investors, entrepreneurs, and often overlooked communities, promoting equity across various sectors such as investing, climate, health care, and education. Too often companies make critical decisions without meaningfully engaging the communities most affected by them. Pharmaceutical companies, for instance, may design and distribute drugs without consulting the patients and communities most impacted, which can lead to mistrust or solutions that miss the realities on the ground. Similarly, large agriculture companies develop products and policies that shape entire food systems yet frequently overlook the voices of farmers who are closest to the land and best positioned to inform sustainable practices. These disconnects erode trust and represent missed opportunities for deeper alignment between business and community needs.

In this chapter, we will start within, exploring those inner spiritual values and principles that define who we are and how we want to show up at work and in life. Above all, we will focus on building bridges and connecting around our shared humanity in all facets of life.

Connecting as Human Beings

My work leading Impact Experience has deepened my appreciation for the importance of this bridge-building when creating ethically driven businesses. Whether in southern West Virginia, New Orleans, or Montgomery, Alabama, I have seen the profound impact of truly understanding the communities and individuals we engage with. During the Impact Experiences we organize, we gather diverse groups—investors, entrepreneurs, community partners—and begin by each sharing something personally meaningful: a symbol or an object. This practice allows us to connect on a human level first, before professional roles define our interactions. Sadly, often such deep human connection rarely occurs in our daily professional lives. Small moments like these open doors to collaborations built on a foundation of mutual understanding and respect, celebrating the fullness of everyone's humanity.

I once facilitated such a dialogue between a former coal miner and a renewable-energy business leader. The coal miner brought a piece of coal to our meeting, not only as a symbol of his livelihood but also of his identity. The renewable energy businessperson, in contrast, presented a solar panel. On the surface, these two individuals could not have looked more different. Yet, as they spoke, it became evident that their core motivations—family, community, a better future—were strikingly similar. This experience helped to spark collaborations that led to job creation initiatives, broadband access collaboration, tourism opportunities, and repurposing of former coal mining land.

This was a defining moment for me because it demonstrated the power of understanding and respecting diverse narratives. Truly listening to another's perspective, even (especially) when it conflicts with your own, can form a bridge beyond industry differences and personal beliefs. Navigating this discomfort and disconnect with open-minded curiosity and openhearted compassion can lead to new cooperation between parties that traditionally view themselves at odds—the kind of cooperation that can innovate models of business growth that benefit everyone.

When I founded Impact Experience, this approach was the driving force. We saw a need for deeper community integration within the business and investment sectors—to foster spaces where authentic connections could flourish alongside profitability. Much of our work has been focused on addressing the fact that (as I write this) fewer than 2 percent of the $82 trillion asset management business is made up of firms led by women and people of color. We engage in work within marginalized communities with the goal of unlocking more capital for founders, investors, and leaders who have been overlooked and underestimated. When we engage deeply with communities, we are better able to address larger societal issues that affect both our work and our personal lives. This opens doors for business and organizational leaders to apply a more spiritual lens toward building an ever-advancing civilization.

Core Spiritual Principles

One of my favorite quotations reflects the South African principle of *Ubuntu*. Although sometimes defined as "humanity," the term directly translates to "I am because we are."

When I was fourteen, I had the unforgettable privilege of speaking at the Commonwealth Day Observance at Westminster Abbey in London, where young representatives of different faith traditions gathered to speak about pressing global issues. I was honored to represent the Bahá'í community and to share reflections on the environment. The service included remarkable addresses from Queen Elizabeth II, Prime Minister Tony Blair, and Archbishop

Desmond Tutu, who had invited an extraordinary choir from South Africa whose voices filled the abbey with power and hope.

Before the event, I made my way over to Archbishop Tutu to greet him with a handshake. Instead, with his trademark twinkle, he waved my hand away, insisting, "No—I want to give you a high five!" That simple joyous gesture, delivered with his warm smile, became an indelible memory. More profoundly, he took a moment to speak of *Ubuntu*—the South African principle that expresses our shared humanity and interdependence—teaching that we belong to one another and that kindness binds us together.

Ten years later, when I was twenty-four and managing the Divest-Invest Philanthropy initiative, I encountered Archbishop Tutu again. I reminded him that we had met a decade earlier and that he had given me a high five. He laughed and said, "Well then, now I will give you a high five—and a hug."

MYSELF AND OTHERS DANCING WITH DESMOND TUTU AT WESTMINSTER ABBEY IN LONDON IN 2004

What can we learn from "I am because we are"? What do we gain by defining humanity in terms of this connection between the personal and the collective—and what does this mean for business? For me, it means acknowledging that, as humans, everything we do as individuals derives from and contributes back to humanity as a whole. It helps me to see our societies and economies not just as systems of commerce but also as the interrelated ecosystems they are.

As socially conscious professionals and leaders, we begin by genuinely engaging with others as human beings, recognizing their needs, aspirations, and motivations. Consultation and collaboration are bedrocks of this approach. In an increasingly polarized world, it is crucial to create spaces where people can come together, despite differing viewpoints. When we invite and celebrate diversity of thought, experience, and background, we forge relationships over division, enriching our communities alongside our companies and organizations. Rachel Robasciotti and Maya Philipson, as cofounders of Adasina Social Capital, have become recognized leaders in bridging the worlds of investing and social justice by aligning investor capital with the needs and priorities of grassroots movements and marginalized communities. Their work centers on mobilizing investors not only to avoid companies perpetuating injustice but also to actively drive systemic change through targeted campaigns on issues such as racial, gender, economic, and climate justice. They engage deeply with communities to understand their key priorities and then build investment campaigns and engagements from there. This bridge-building approach amplifies the voices of those most affected by inequity using community-sourced data, coalition-based advocacy, and transparent exclusion lists.

Robasciotti is also intentional about integrating her spiritual practice into her professional life, emphasizing the transformative power of deep presence and inquiry both in her leadership and in

Adasina's impact work. Her commitment to mindful, values-driven engagement helps create a culture of listening and reflective action, strengthening the authenticity and integrity of Adasina's bridge-building efforts between investors and social justice campaigns.

It is essential to reach beyond our familiar circles and to make the effort to understand the perspectives and needs of others, especially those who have been historically marginalized or overlooked. In the rush of our daily routines, we often forget to lay the groundwork for bridge-building in our interactions, which can lead to misunderstandings. When we recognize how diversity enriches companies and communities, we can instead nurture and learn from these connections—and avoid the negative consequences of running our businesses in ways that exploit, extracts from, and misunderstand local communities and other stakeholders.

When we understand that "I am because we are," we remember that connections are not just some abstract ideal; they are vital for any successful, long-term human enterprise. This idea of bridge-building resonates deeply with me because of its ability to connect seemingly distinct spheres—business, community, and personal values. To me, the topic feels urgent, rooted in my core belief in the oneness of humanity, a principle foundational to my work and worldview.

Shoghi Effendi, the Guardian of the Bahá'í Faith, said,

> We cannot segregate the human heart from the environment outside us and say that once one of these is reformed, everything will be improved. Man is organic with the world. His inner life molds the environment and is itself also deeply affected by it. The one acts upon the other and every abiding change in the life of man is the result of these mutual reactions.[3]

As business leaders who care about impact, we must first define our own spiritual values and principles—for example, my focus on bridge-building, rooted in the spiritual principles of *Ubuntu*. Next, we are called to integrate those values and principles into our work while being mindful of how those values and principles intersect with the communities and ecosystems in which we work as well as the broader impact we leave behind.

People, Purpose, and Performance

Spiritual beliefs, often relegated to our personal affairs, can powerfully redefine business strategies and investment approaches. Many spiritually and socially conscious investors express frustration with the relentless push for immediate, short-term profitability. This motive is exacerbated by the fact that publicly traded companies report on a quarterly cycle, which can complicate longer-term planning. When investors pause to reflect on the long-term impacts of their choices, they have the time to align more closely with their core values, often prioritizing sustainability, equity, and well-being over purely short-term financial returns.

The shift is not limited to investors. Companies such as Barry-Wehmiller exemplify this alignment by emphasizing values rooted in an expressed leadership philosophy of people, purpose, and performance. Bob Chapman, chairman of the board of Barry-Wehmiller, incorporated these values into his leadership strategy after a personal experience led him to reflect on his mission previously as CEO.

From there, he made a deliberate effort to examine his own personal values and better integrate those into his business strategy moving forward, transforming the company into a model of people-centered leadership. For the next thirty years of Chapman's ongoing leadership, his emphasis on people and purpose led to exceptional performance as well as a deep fulfillment among his employees and company leaders alike. Through embracing a culture of truly human leadership, Barry-Wehmiller created a robust organization that delivers value to all its stakeholders—from its almost thirteen thousand global team members and their families to their customers, shareholders, vendors, and suppliers and to the communities in which they conduct business. Since committing to this unique, caring culture, the company has also grown from a $10 million revenue business into a global $3 billion revenue organization.[4]

When I interviewed Chapman for this book, he told me how he and his team realized their profound responsibility for the lives entrusted to them as leaders. He also talked about how their leadership impacted not only the time people spent at work but also their health and family lives. Chapman explained that, initially, he saw the thirteen thousand individuals within his company—engineers, accountants, hourly workers, and others—as mere functions contributing to business success. His company was modern, efficient, and nice by conventional standards, as it related to employee benefits and customer service, but it lacked deeper human connection.

What exactly was the catalyst that transformed how Chapman viewed leadership and business and set Barry-Wehmiller on this trajectory of enlightened growth? It all goes back to one fateful summer evening when he attended the wedding of a friend. Watching the ceremony, Chapman reflected on his own life and family—and was struck by a sudden realization. It occurred to him that just like the bride and groom uniting their lives that day, each one of his employees was someone's precious child, entrusted to him for forty hours each week. He understood that how he treated them would not only shape their professional lives but also ripple into their health, family dynamics, and personal relationships. This epiphany became the foundation of his commitment to validating everyone's worth and ensuring that they knew their contributions mattered.

Guided by this revelation, Chapman overhauled his leadership philosophy, embedding empathy and care into the core of his organization. He founded an internal education program called the Barry-Wehmiller University to teach skills such as empathetic listening, recognition, and a culture of service—skills that transitioned managers into true leaders. Remarkably, 95 percent of feedback from employees highlighted the impact these skills and practices had on their personal lives, especially when it came to improving relationships with spouses and children. Chapman's philosophy endures because it went far beyond empty lip service about company values. By incorporating this approach into every aspect of the company's training, education, and service, Chapman created a genuinely fulfilling workplace culture that inspired deep engagement among his team.

His organization became a model for transforming workplace culture, inspiring leaders such as Simon Sinek, the visionary author and speaker best known for popularizing the concept behind his global bestseller *Start with Why*. In a podcast produced by Barry-Wehmiller, Sinek said,

"I imagine a world in which the vast majority of people wake up inspired, feel safe wherever they are, and end the day fulfilled by the work that they do. Bob Chapman, legendary CEO of manufacturing company Barry-Wehmiller, has done more than most other leaders to bring that vision to life."[5] Chapman's journey demonstrates the power of human-centered leadership to heal the brokenness in workplaces and beyond, creating a legacy of compassion and connection, all rooted in our common humanity.

"I am because we are." Regardless of anyone's personal family dynamics, viewing every individual you meet as someone's precious child highlights the collective ties that bind us all beneath the surface. As Chapman has demonstrated, applying that insight to business strategy enriches everyone involved—both materially and personally.

"While proud of achieving more than 18 percent compound annual return for its shareholders since 1987," Sinek wrote in *Start with Why*, "Bob Chapman and his team had come to see that true success should be measured by the way they touch the lives of people."[6]

Over the years, Barry-Wehmiller has acquired more than one hundred companies. They tested and refined these leadership practices within each of these companies to ensure that these principles become firmly integrated into the DNA of the Barry-Wehmiller global leadership practices.

The Ripple Effect

This more spiritual approach to business addresses stark evidence of need: widening disparities in wealth, environmental degradation, and the chaos of social fragmentation.

There are several examples from the global academic community that have been creating spaces to engage more around spirituality in recent decades. Institutions such as the Stanford University Center for Compassion and Altruism Research and Education[7] and the Massachusetts Institute of Technology Dalai Lama Center for Ethics and Transformative Values[8] both integrate spiritual and ethical considerations into their work, blending science with humanistic values. For example, the Center for Compassion and Altruism Research and Education website has compiled a "Compassion Database" where you can search hundreds of scholarly papers related to how human compassion impacts everything from corporate health care leadership to economic systems to employee satisfaction and more.[9]

This perspective also expands far beyond the ivory tower of academia as more businesses incorporate values-driven practices. Consider the growth of impact investing, which channels capital into projects and companies that generate measurable social and environmental benefits alongside financial returns. From renewable energy initiatives to affordable housing projects, these investments demonstrate that financial performance and positive impact are not mutually exclusive. The Global Impact Investing Network published a report in 2024 estimating that the impact investing market has grown since 2019 by a 21 percent compound annual growth rate, with organizations managing more than $1.571 trillion in assets under management.[10]

In the corporate world, companies that prioritize purpose alongside profit are rewriting the narrative of success. One such pioneering company is Patagonia. As part of our Business Climate Finance Initiative within Impact Experience, my team and I have collaborated with Patagonia to support and reinforce the continued integration of social responsibility into their treasury and investments.

This certified B Corporation[11] is known for both its high-quality outdoor gear and its commitment to using sustainable materials, reducing waste, and supporting environmental causes. From the beginning, founder Yvon Chouinard made a choice to grow slowly and organically. For a long time, the company refused external investments, preferring to invest their resources not just for profit but also for purpose.

On September 14, 2022, Patagonia announced a new ownership structure, as the Chouinard family transferred all its ownership to two new entities: the Patagonia Purpose Trust and the Holdfast Collective. Through this arrangement, every dollar that is not reinvested into Patagonia now gets distributed as dividends to protect the planet. One hundred percent of profits not reinvested into the business (approximately $100 million annually as of this book's publication) are now distributed as dividends to the Holdfast Collective to fund climate and biodiversity protection and to fight the environmental crisis.[12]

In their press release announcing the move, the company explained that the Patagonia Purpose Trust would now own all the voting stock of the company (2 percent of the total stock). According to the release, the whole idea was to "create a more permanent legal structure to enshrine Patagonia's purpose and values. It will help ensure that there is never deviation from the intent of the founder and to facilitate what the company continues to do best: demonstrate as a for-profit business that capitalism can work for the planet."[13]

It went on to quote Chouinard:

> It's been a half-century since we began our experiment in responsible business. If we have any hope of a thriving planet fifty years from now, it demands all of us doing all we can with the resources we have. As the business leader I never wanted to be, I am doing my part. Instead of extracting value from nature and transforming it into wealth, we are using the wealth Patagonia creates to protect the source. We're making Earth our only shareholder. I am dead serious about saving this planet.[14]

One of the most rewarding aspects of my work involves collaborating with organizations that, inspired by Patagonia's ownership structure, have integrated similar models within their own businesses. One example is an asset management firm, and another is a hospitality group. Both created structures that bolster and preserve their values while actively engaging employees in the process. This creates a self-perpetuating culture of impact that outlives the founders' active involvement. This stepwise ripple effect is exactly how corporate choices can make practical, concrete steps that impact other businesses and communities—which then do the same in turn.

Moving Toward Harmony

Let's engage in a thought exercise. Imagine this: You are the CEO of a company managing an investment fund. Your team has just been presented with an opportunity to invest in a fast-growing supplier offering significant financial returns within the next couple of years. At first glance, it seems like an obvious choice—an investment that could boost portfolio performance and deliver impressive financial gains. But before you approve the deal, you take a moment to pause and reflect.

Sitting at your desk, you ask yourself, *Does this investment align with our company's higher purpose? How will it influence the trust and confidence of our employees and stakeholders, who believe in our commitment to conscious investing? Most importantly, what ripple effect will this decision have on the broader society and environment?*

As you dig deeper, you uncover troubling details about the supplier's operations, suggesting poor labor conditions and environmental negligence, both of which contradict the principles of equity and sustainability you hold dear. The potential financial returns come into sharp contrast with the moral cost of aligning with a company that undermines your values.

Instead of dismissing the opportunity outright, you shift your perspective and ask, *How could we respond to this opportunity in a way that serves a higher purpose? Can we influence the supplier to improve their practices as a condition of our investment, fostering change that benefits their workers and the planet? Or should we seek out different investment opportunities that better align with our ethical standards while still delivering strong returns?*

In that moment, you realize that conscious investing is not just about maximizing profits—it's also about honoring your principles, fostering trust, and creating a positive legacy. By making decisions rooted in a higher purpose, you ensure that your investments resonate beyond mere finances, uplifting everyone connected to your work.

The framework presented in this book will equip you with tools to create a more conscientious and holistic approach to investing, leading with impact, and both founding and transforming businesses that inspire and change the world.

The Bahá'í writings state that "until material achievements, physical accomplishments, and human virtues are reinforced by spiritual perfections, luminous qualities, and characteristics of mercy, no fruit or result shall issue therefrom, nor will the happiness of the world of humanity, which is the ultimate aim, be attained."[15]

Let this call to action resonate deeply: to invest with intention, lead with integrity, and embody the harmony we seek to create.

REFLECTION QUESTIONS

- Take a moment to consider your own personal intersection of ethics, spirituality, and business. What are three to five values that come to mind when you think about how these elements align for you?
- How will you stick to your values in decisions about investments, marketing, culture, growth, and the company's overall business practices?
- Have you cultivated a culture at all levels of the organization that encourages bridge-building through meaningful discussions and reflection? Have you also ensured that this culture of dialogue and inclusion influences your decision-making?
- Do you have policies and processes in place to support this mindful, reflective, and ethical culture as well as the growth you're trying to promote?
- What lessons could you take from the Patagonia example as you look at preserving the spiritual purpose, direction, and legacy of your company?
- What are some ways you reinforce your business practices with spiritual perfections and luminous qualities that promote your continued success?

CHAPTER 2

A Renaissance of Optimism and Transformation

Day by day, what you choose, what you think,
and what you do is who you become.

—**HERACLITUS**, ANCIENT GREEK PHILOSOPHER

In an era filled with pessimism, fake news, toxic leadership, and a broken world, precious few stories seem to focus on optimism, connection, and progress. These corrosive forces, driven home by misinformation and distrust, often make our world feel like a fragile house of cards sitting on top of disillusionment. But amid this chaos lies a quiet revolution of optimism and change that I believe is on the rise—one underpinned by a conviction that it is possible to build a new world oriented toward the betterment of humanity and the planet.

Misinformation destroys trust, just as greed erodes the long-term stability of organizations and stalls societal progress. According to McKinsey's post–COVID-19 data, an increasing number of workers around the world say their mental health deteriorated during the pandemic, and these same workers are more likely to experience economic instability and divisive rhetoric.[1]

Studies from Deloitte reveal a deep distrust of corporate leadership, along with growing pressure from employees, who increasingly demand transparency, empathy, and purpose-driven action. Privacy breaches, misinformation, and companies falling short of their promises have become all too common.

One 2022 Deloitte analysis revealed that three major (unspecified) global companies, valued at over $10 billion each, all saw their market value plummet by between 20 and 56 percent due to perceived mistrust, amounting to a staggering $70 billion in total losses.[2] Often these businesses initially appear successful, with leaders assuming their organizations are trusted—until an unforeseen breach of trust occurs. In some cases, the concept of trust is not even on the radar until it is too late.

The consequences of losing stakeholder trust can be devastating. Loss of trust often leads to decreased employee morale, lower productivity, and higher turnover rates, which directly impact organizational stability. Moreover, companies may face reputational damage that erodes customer loyalty and investor confidence, potentially resulting in declining sales and stock value. Breaches in trust have precipitated costly legal challenges, regulatory fines, and, in extreme cases, the collapse of entire businesses. Beyond immediate financial consequences, a damaged relationship with stakeholders hampers collaboration and innovation, creating long-term barriers to sustainable growth. Recovering trust demands transparent communication, accountability, and concrete action plans, but the reactive cost of neglecting these efforts often far outweighs the proactive investment in maintaining strong stakeholder relationships. Many senior executives recognize this need to build or rebuild trust in their organizations. However, they often struggle to understand exactly how trust can be earned.

Meanwhile, the past few years have witnessed a mounting

cultural and economic backlash to ESG (environmental, social, and governance) and sustainability initiatives. The backlash is driven by a complex array of factors: political polarization, concerns over regulatory overreach, fear that ESG strategies undermine traditional business performance, and allegations of greenwashing and virtue signaling by companies. At its core, many critics argue that ESG distracts from financial performance and undermines shareholder primacy.

This fragmentation is echoed globally, with North America experiencing especially acute polarization compared to other regions. As a result, executives now see regulatory fragmentation and government intervention as new front lines of the debate, and many companies are quietly rebranding or scaling back public-facing ESG language, even as they continue to pursue elements of sustainability internally.

For those opposed to ESG, the values that rise to the fore are often framed as fiduciary responsibility, market efficiency, and the primacy of shareholder value. However, a compelling case can be made that sound sustainability practices can, in fact, reinforce financial resilience and reputation. This offers returns—both tangible and intangible—that benefit shareholders and society alike over the long run. Contrary to the zero-sum framing that often dominates the public debate, the intersection of spirituality, investing, and business reminds us that expanding the definition of *value* to include purpose, meaning, and stewardship may offer the most abundant path forward, both for individual companies and for the broader world.

Furthermore, recent studies reveal a surge of individuals seeking deeper connection and meaning. For example, a 2022 working paper by Brookings showed that relationships are the most important determinant of meaningfulness at work and in the business arena.[3] Moreover, those who feel a strong sense of relatedness and trust—and thus derive greater meaning from their jobs—are more likely to increase their effort, engagement, and productivity at work.

Optimism, in particular, helps both individuals and businesses to flourish. Harvard Health's research underscores the link between optimism and well-being, showing that optimistic individuals are 30 percent less likely to suffer from heart disease and tend to live longer than their pessimistic counterparts.[4]

A New Paradigm: From Fear to Flourishing

Niren Chaudhary, formerly the CEO of Panera Brands and Bread, is known for his human-centric approach to business and leadership, one that emphasizes character and values. Chaudhary's insights and actions reveal how a focus on purpose can actually drive up profits, challenging the notion of a trade-off between the two.

When the COVID-19 pandemic struck and disrupted every aspect of life, Chaudhary looked for opportunities not just to sustain his own business but also to serve communities in need. He was deeply committed to the idea that profit and purpose could coexist, and he saw disruption as an opportunity rather than as an impediment. On the consumer side, Panera responded swiftly by creating new offerings such as the Panera Grocery business, expanding its digital e-commerce channels with pickup available at every restaurant and turbocharging its delivery business.

One day, Chaudhary came across a piece of news that deeply troubled him regarding many schools in Ohio, and across the country, that had shut down, so millions of children no longer had access to the meals they normally received each day at school. He wondered whether Panera could step in to help solve this urgent problem in a way that created a win-win outcome for children, families, and the business. The idea was simple but powerful—children could come to Panera stores to receive their school meals.

To make this vision real, Chaudhary reached out directly to the governor of Ohio to understand the issue more closely and to explore potential solutions. The US Department of Agriculture (USDA) was funding school meal programs, but the per-child budget was extremely low—just five to six dollars per day. Panera's team rose to the challenge with price-led innovation, finding a way to provide nutritious meals that met USDA specifications while staying within the strict cost constraints. It became a win for the children who regained access to nourishing food, a win for the government that fulfilled its mandate, and a win for Panera, which could continue to serve communities in meaningful ways amid the crisis.

The team then worked through the logistics of designing and launching the program across Ohio. It quickly drew national recognition, with the USDA expressing pride in the partnership. In fact, during a White House COVID-19 briefing, the program was highlighted by the US president as an example of an effective public-private partnership. Chaudhary was invited to speak about the initiative in that high-profile setting. He recalled, in an interview with me, how nervous he was that day—his throat was dry as he prepared to describe the program—but also how inspired he felt to share the innovative work Panera had done to meet a critical need during such a turbulent time.

During our conversation, Chaudhary went on to say that he views decisions through the lens of whether they are brand accretive, people accretive, and culture accretive, with the understanding that these factors can also be monetized for company growth, either right away or in the future. Chaudhary underscores the importance of acceptance, forgiveness, self-love, and then hope as key elements in navigating challenges and fostering a positive mindset. Although the notion of infinite economic growth may present unsustainable social and ecological costs, Chaudhary does believe that some things—such as wisdom, cooperation, and good ideas—really are infinite.

Transformation begins with a release of old paradigms based on fear, scarcity, and control. Instead, we have an opportunity to adopt a mindset—and practice—of resilience, abundance, purpose, and even transformation. According to a 2024 McKinsey study, companies and investors who embrace and apply this mindset regularly report higher employee engagement, improved financial performance, and more resilient organizational cultures.[5] This report suggests that individuals who exhibit both high resilience and adaptability are more than three times as likely to report strong engagement at work and are nearly four times more likely to demonstrate innovative behaviors. Dr. Anna Yusim, an award-winning Stanford- and Yale-educated psychiatrist and executive coach, brings these same insights to her clients. She works with Fortune 500 CEOs, Olympic athletes, and other high-profile professionals to help them achieve greater impact, purpose, and joy.

In our interview, Yusim emphasized that the strength of a business ultimately reflects the consciousness of its leaders. Her work focuses on heart-opening, a practice aimed at helping individuals connect to something greater than themselves, expand their consciousness, and balance intellectual rigor with intuitive wisdom. This process encourages cultivating vulnerability and compassion, allowing people to move beyond fear-based reactions toward greater emotional resilience and authentic connection with others. She knows that active listening builds trust and fosters collaboration, that inclusion and adaptability cultivate spaces where diverse perspectives can flourish, and that empathy reinforces our shared humanity. These attributes all lend themselves to the cooperative spirit of resilience and transformation that she instills in her clients.

Yusim believes that leaders who operate from a heart-centered, intuitive space make more impactful and authentic decisions, not only for themselves but also for their organizations. This philosophy aligns with investing in values-driven, socially conscious companies that embody purpose and mission at their core. Through coaching, deep contemplation, and reflection, it is possible to emerge out of the shadows of fear and develop a leadership lens founded on the spirit of optimism.

Cultivating Optimism

Even if you're a person who struggles to cultivate optimism, just a few small adjustments have the possibility of improving your outlook on life. Research shows that we can cultivate optimism through simple practices, such as imagining the best possible outcomes in different areas of our lives.[6]

Infusing optimism into the often daunting world of investments is no small feat, yet that is exactly what Daryn Dodson aims to do with his work. As the managing partner of Illumen Capital,[7] Dodson leads an extraordinary asset management firm investing in impact-oriented private equity and venture capital funds, with a unique focus on reducing bias related to race and gender. In addition to his work at Illumen, Dodson serves on the board of Ben & Jerry's and previously worked with the Calvert Funds.

I asked Dodson how he maintains this sense of optimism and possibility. His response was deeply rooted in history and spirituality. He reflected on the vast reserves of strength embedded in spiritual traditions—songs and messages passed down from ancestors, grounded in the theologian Thomas Fuller's famous belief that it is always darkest before the dawn.

Dodson also invoked the sacrifices of leaders such as Martin Luther King, Jr., Nelson Mandela, and Frederick Douglass, emphasizing that the work Illumen Capital does today is only possible because of what these figures endured. Dodson described the privilege of advancing equity in a relatively free society, contrasted with the atrocities endured by these historical leaders as well as by those still living under violent oppression today. For him, this mission is not only a professional calling but also a profound act of faith, gratitude, and alignment with values. This broader awareness helps Dodson sustain his sense of joy and purpose in the face of systemic challenges. As he put it,

> Although I am profoundly grateful for the opportunity to do this work without the constant threat of violence that others in history endured, I am also mindful of those who continue to live under such threats today. My heart goes out to them as fellow members of the human family. The struggle for justice and equity persists, and I feel deeply honored to contribute to this mission in a way that is aligned with my values, faith, and purpose. Each day, I am reminded of the privilege it is to engage in this work and the importance of carrying it forward.

Reflecting on Dodson's powerful insights on hope, I am struck by how anyone can embrace and apply these fundamental tenets, regardless of their spiritual practices or beliefs. His words inspire me with hope for the future of humanity. We will come back to this theme of hope in Chapter 4.

If you struggle with optimism, you're not alone, but it is possible to shift your mindset with the right focus and practice. Just ask Christiana Figueres. Figueres is a Costa Rican diplomat and environmentalist best known for her leadership as executive secretary of the United Nations Framework Convention on Climate Change from 2010 to 2016, where she played a crucial role in orchestrating the historic 2015 Paris Agreement to address climate change. Figueres powerfully reframes optimism as a deliberate input—an active choice and a moral commitment rather than a passive hope. She calls this stubborn optimism, a gritty, relentless determination to keep moving forward despite daunting challenges. Figueres reminds us that impossible is not a fact; it is an attitude. This mindset transforms the impossible into a beacon of possible, lighting the way for visionary leadership that designs a better future.

I had the opportunity to take part in a program that Figueres organized in collaboration with Plum Village, bringing together climate leaders from around the world to engage around the intersection of spirituality and climate. Plum Village, founded in 1982 by Zen Master Thích Nhất Hạnh in southwest France, is Europe's largest Buddhist monastery and an international mindfulness practice center. Much of the focus of our program was on how we can live in greater harmony with ourselves and the Earth through mindful living.

In the intersection of spirituality and business, Figueres's philosophy invites us to embody a regenerative approach grounded in both realism and hope, actively showing that a different and better path is within reach. This optimism fuels creativity and collective action, anchoring investment strategies that prioritize long-term impact and legacy over short-term gain. Choosing optimism in this way aligns with a spiritual call to cocreate futures that honor both present needs and the well-being of generations to come.

Strategies for Optimism in Leadership

As a business leader or team member, your mindset significantly influences not only your personal success but also the morale and productivity of those around you. For this exercise, imagine you are leading a team at a midsize organization. Sales have slumped, and the energy in the office feels heavy. You are preparing for a critical meeting to brainstorm solutions, and tensions are high. Here are some strategies that might help you lead with clarity and positivity:

- **Accentuate the positive.** Before stepping into the meeting, take five minutes to jot down some recent wins. Perhaps a team member landed a small but promising client or a new product received great feedback. Reflect on the factors, such as team collaboration or innovative thinking, that contributed to these moments of progress. Start the meeting by asking your team how you might build on these strengths, and invite everyone to celebrate and learn from small wins, even amid recent and ongoing challenges. Sharing and discussing these glimmers with your team at the start of the meeting can help set a constructive tone.
- **Treat doubts with care.** When doubts about the meeting's outcome arise, notice them as part of the natural landscape of your mind—not as obstacles to be bulldozed but as signals to slow down, breathe, and recenter. Focus on positive, grounding thoughts, interactions, and activities rather than giving into rumination and doubt. Perhaps an uplifting playlist can bring you into the flow of your work, or a conversation with a trusted mentor can help you find your balance. The idea is not to banish negative thoughts but rather to carry both realism and hope into the room. Chaudhary talks about practicing resilience through

acceptance, forgiveness, self-love, and hope—tending to his inner life much like a gardener tending a beloved plot, knowing that all feelings, even the unwelcome ones, have their season and their place.

- **Act locally.** Acknowledging that you cannot control global market trends, instead focus on a tangible step your team can take, such as launching a targeted local marketing campaign. Pick an initiative that not only feels achievable but also empowers the team with a sense of purpose and momentum.
- **Go easy on yourself.** After the meeting, resist the powerful urge to replay perceived missteps in your mind. Instead, recognize the effort you and your team put into finding solutions. Treat yourself kindly—maybe that means taking a walk, eating a healthy meal, or scheduling time to rest. Self-compassion allows you to maintain resilience and approach the next challenge with fresh energy.

Practice Mindfulness

Scott Shickler cofounded 7 Mindsets in 2009 with Jeff Waller. Their company partners with schools to implement its pre–K to twelfth grade mindset-based learning curriculum. From 2009 to 2022, Shickler served as CEO of 7 Mindsets, helping the company expand its reach and inspire millions of students and educators to live lives of passion, purpose, and joy. Today, 7 Mindsets stands as the nation's leading provider of multitiered mindset-based and mental health learning solutions. Shickler returned to the role of CEO in July 2024 to lead the organization into its next phase of growth.

Shickler informed me about his unique approaches to cultivating optimism and hope, particularly through the lens of his magic wand practice. He and Waller separately cofounded a charitable organization called the Magic Wand Foundation. Shickler shared how the symbolic presence of a magic wand on his desk serves as a daily reminder to expand his thinking and intentions. For Shickler, waving the wand is not about wishful thinking. Instead, it is an exercise in imagining possibilities beyond the constraints of limited human perspectives. This creative prop encourages the practice of hope by indulging expansive desires—while staying deeply grounded in gratitude and realism. Shickler emphasized that without gratitude for what we already have—our current circumstances, accomplishments, and who we are in the present—hope feels fleeting and ephemeral. Without the right perspective, present and future gains can be overshadowed by doubts, fears, and dissatisfaction. He described gratitude as a daily discipline, reflecting each night on what he is thankful for that day and allowing this ritual to deepen over time.

Shickler also shared a powerful mental shift to counteract negative or fear-based thinking. He explained how he actively identifies pessimistic thoughts, such as anxieties about the future or self-doubt, and consciously reframes them into positive, empowering alternatives. This flipping-the-switch exercise fosters a mindset of optimism and builds resilience in the face of life's uncertainties. Through these practices, Shickler exemplifies how intentionality, gratitude, and an openhearted belief in possibility can help cultivate lasting hope, even amid challenging circumstances.

The key is to find a mindfulness or gratitude practice that resonates with you. Start small. Even just one to three minutes a day of mindfulness can make a huge difference. Tomorrow, before leaving work behind at the end of the day, take a few moments to stop and focus on your breath. Acknowledge the day's challenges without judgment, and bring your attention to the present moment. This practice helps you leave the stress of work behind and arrive home ready to recharge. If you find it hard to sit still, try movement practices like gentle yoga videos or simply take a nice slow, meditative walk without music or distractions. You can also explore resources such as guided meditation apps or workplace mindfulness workshops.

Although incorporating small mindfulness practices into your day-to-day is the ultimate aim, it can sometimes help to get away from the bustle and noise for a more extended, intentional retreat. Stacy Brown-Philpot, founder and managing partner of Cherryrock Capital, discovered this firsthand during a six-day silent meditation retreat she took after leaving her CEO role at Taskrabbit, a digital platform connecting freelance laborers with local demand. After the company was sold to IKEA, Brown-Philpot decided to take a break and delve into a discipline of silence and introspection. Initially apprehensive about being alone and disconnected, she discovered during the retreat a deep rest her body needed and a centeredness that shifted her perspective. As she shared on the podcast *Masters of Scale*, the experience helped Brown-Philpot realize that the world continues without her constant presence. This allowed her to listen inwardly, say no to outside expectations, and clearly determine her next steps—ultimately leading her to cofound a venture fund, Cherryrock Capital. The retreat offered a powerful example of how stepping back through meditation can provide pivotal insight for career and life decisions.[8]

A Story of Enoughness

One of the greatest saboteurs of optimism and transformation is this idea that we're falling behind or not doing enough. This can take the form of impostor syndrome and constant comparison to colleagues or made-up ideals. It can be easy to forget how to slow down, celebrate our wins, show gratitude, and above all, connect with those around us and with the present moment.

This reminds me of a story my grandmother, Stella Maria Forte (known to us as Gags) used to share. When she was younger, she ran a fashion store in London. One day a stranger entered the store, a woman who looked weary and depressed. My grandmother could have politely ignored the woman's obvious despair, carried out some robotic sale, or even shooed the woman away when she lingered too long, staring listlessly at the shelves.

Instead, my grandmother gently approached the woman and asked her if something was wrong. This unleashed a torrent of tears, as the woman confessed that she had hit her lowest point—and in fact had been thinking of taking her own life. My grandmother sat down with this woman and talked with her for hours that day, listening and providing comforting words. That woman later came back to the shop and thanked her, insisting that those moments of unexpected kindness and connection had saved her life.

My grandmother would often say, "If I did nothing else in my life but save that woman, my life was complete."

This perspective of enoughness resonated deeply with me and became a guiding inspiration in my own journey to make a difference, as a business leader and as a human being. My grandmother's unwavering belief in the value of even a single act of life-changing support motivated me to work at a youth-to-youth helpline from the ages of thirteen to seventeen. There I had the opportunity to support my peers who were struggling with suicidal thoughts, carrying forward her legacy of compassion and reinforcing my own belief that every life touched holds profound meaning.

Embracing the idea that we are enough just as we are challenges the relentless pursuit of what's next. It encourages us to appreciate the profound impact of what we have already accomplished. Last year, a dear friend echoed this sentiment in a birthday card, writing, "I hope you can internalize the idea that you have already done so many amazing things, and everything else is extra." Internalizing this liberating thought, although sometimes challenging, fuels my sense of optimism.

I now invite you to consider the same idea, to acknowledge not just your achievements and accolades but also all the ways, big and small, that you have improved the lives of others, even just for one day.

This is not to say that we should become complacent. If you are a founder, a leader, or an investor, you are likely energized by growth, goals, and fast-paced environments. It is still critical to take care of your fiscal bottom line, as long as you also stay mindful of the enlightened bottom line, measured by appreciation for this experience of life and connection with one another. We have an opportunity to be more optimistic, more responsive, and more resilient—and, I think, more capable of the kind of transformative experiences and impact we can have as openhearted leaders who prioritize connections over mere transactions.

Resilience, Equanimity, and the Inner Critic

Often people conflate resilience with the ability to stand strong, fight back, and endure. But far from being rigid and unyielding, resilience is elastic. It stretches and bends and responds.

Because we cannot create a controlled, stress-free environment in life (or not for long), resilience is a necessary learned skill and ongoing practice. According to the Stress & Resilience Institute, resilience is not about eliminating stress but about learning how to bounce back.[9]

Whitney Johnson, author of the book *Disrupt Yourself: Master Relentless Change and Speed Up Your Learning Curve*, believes anyone can train in resilience to better deal with change and rise up stronger.[10] Johnson encourages leaders to engage in self-reflection exercises such as journaling. In particular, she writes about the power of embracing your imperfections and transforming your inner critic. The aim is not perfection but honest, connective expression.[11]

Psychologist Dr. Anna Yusim agrees. When I interviewed her for this book, she highlighted the importance of maintaining an open heart, even in the face of setbacks or betrayals. True resilience, she said, lies in learning from these experiences, adapting, and even protecting yourself in the moment—without hardening your heart or suppressing your ability to feel and trust.

Of course, in a rapid-paced (and often legitimately threatening) world, it's all about striking a balance—being discerning and setting healthy boundaries while also remaining compassionate. Through this, leaders can not only navigate adversity but also emerge stronger, fostering a culture of resilience that maintains authenticity and connection.

In cultivating resilience, another topic that often comes up is the practice of equanimity. Equanimity can be defined as a state of composed mental calmness or grace under fire. It's the ability to allow the difficulties to be there, without letting them dominate our experience or hijack our emotions.

This state of evenness and balanced calm can be difficult to maintain. It takes the ability to accept disappointment, discomfort, and even danger with the right perspective. If we can accept these scenarios with a clear head and an even temper, we become more effective, resilient leaders and humans. Here are some ways to cultivate equanimity and resilience within:

- **Reflective practices:** Integrating reflective practices such as daily journaling, quiet walks, and meditation into your leadership style can help maintain your inner balance.
- **Mindfulness:** Mindfulness is not just about sitting and watching yourself breathe. It's also about nurturing a grounded awareness of the moment—even stressful, uncomfortable, overwhelming ones. By simply pausing, taking a breath, and noticing whatever thoughts, emotions, and events arise in that moment—without judgment or resistance—you can strengthen your capacity for equanimity. The following are some simple practices to get you started:

- Sit comfortably and take a few deep breaths, bringing your attention gently to the present moment and your body sensations. Imagine a time when you felt balanced and even-minded, or visualize a solid mountain symbolizing strength and stability. Notice how this mindful reflection and/or visualization feels inside.
- Reflect on a recent challenge that made equanimity difficult. Acknowledge and accept the situation as it is, without judgment, even if it is unpleasant. Repeat phrases such as "Things are as they are; I can be with things as they are" or "May I accept myself just as I am." This can sometimes be challenging (it often is for me!), but with more practice, it gets easier.
- Practice mindful breathing by focusing on the rise and fall of your breath. When distractions or strong emotions arise, gently note them with the phrase "Ah, right now it's like this," then return your attention to the breath, fostering nonreactive awareness.

- Use simple breathing exercises such as the 4-7-8 breath (inhale for four seconds, hold for seven, exhale for eight) to help calm the nervous system and support a balanced mind.
- Engage in brief mindfulness mini-exercises such as one minute of focused breathing. Or take a moment to consciously observe an object near you. Maybe a paperweight on your desk or a cup of tea in your hand. Notice the textures, colors, and shapes, as though tracing the object in your mind. Run your fingers over it, noticing the feel and temperature. Taking just a few seconds to examine something in this present moment can help anchor your attention and reset a mental spiral or emotional response, fostering more equanimity in daily life.

These exercises help cultivate a more balanced, accepting mind that can meet life's ups and downs with calmness and grace. Repeating them regularly builds the capacity to remain steady amid changing circumstances.

As you deepen your mindfulness practice, you may notice something else wreaking havoc with your decision-making process as a leader: the inner critic. It is the voice that doubts and second-guesses everything you do, from the outfit you chose to the decision you made at the board meeting. It may even pipe up during meditation to tell you that you're wasting your time, just sitting there breathing. But as important as that inner critic may want to feel, this voice is often not helping you lead or progress. Most of the time, it just zaps your energy, courage, and morale.

Again, awareness is the first step. How often has your inner critic spoken up today—holding you back, doubting your abilities, or even judging others? Is it running wild, hindering your growth as a leader? Perhaps you've never fully acknowledged or challenged this relentless voice, but this might be the time to take control.

Instead of trying to deny or disown this voice, befriending the inner critic—a practice endorsed by Susan Brady, author of *Mastering Your Inner Critic and 7 Other High Hurdles to Advancement*—can help you transcend self-doubt and empower yourself.[12] Self-empowerment comes from accepting self-doubts, then reframing our inner dialogue in more positive terms. This helps us observe the inner critic alongside other thoughts, including those of gratitude and hope. We can acknowledge the fear of failure as well as the excitement about starting something new. By tolerating the inner critic without letting it run the show, we can choose which thoughts to focus on and raise ourselves into states of optimism and action in both our professional and our personal lives.

Brady shares powerful, hard-earned insights that can help you transform that inner voice, replacing self-doubt with actionable, empowering solutions. Start by asking yourself the following:

- **Do I know what I want?** Overcome uncertainty and gain clarity about your goals by embracing honesty and authenticity. Get into the habit of asking this question when you find yourself living on autopilot, people-pleasing, or feeling confused.
- **What if it all works out?** Your inner critic loves a good what-if—but mainly when it has to do with doubts and fears. As leaders, we do have to assess risks and create contingency plans. But after examining the worst-case possibilities, allow yourself to imagine possible scenarios, too, including the best-case outcomes.
- **How do I ask for what I need?** You're allowed to express yourself clearly and assertively, without hedging or

apologizing. Tap into your relationships and networks to secure the support you need to achieve anything.

- **Why do I feel the need to do it all?** Let go of the need to prove yourself by doing too much. Learn to empower yourself and others while focusing on what truly matters.

Purpose-driven leadership requires making peace with our inner critic, keeping it in its place (not in the driver's seat), and leading with freedom. With these strategies, you can move forward with confidence, both as a leader and in your daily decisions, whether they involve investments, your business, or your personal life.

The rekindling of optimism challenges us to reenvision what is achievable—not just for ourselves but also for society. When business and investing align with a higher purpose and spirituality, we can collectively cocreate a future that reflects optimism, resilience, and the flourishing of all.

Next, we'll explore real-life examples of leaders who have embraced the inner challenge of spiritual work to lead from a space of higher consciousness and how they are fostering hope and innovation and generating success. When we embrace hope and optimism, we can transform our mindsets, our business cultures, and the impact of our work on the world.

The challenge, as we'll see in chapter 3, is to take inventory of our values and apply those more directly to our leadership choices. This not only opens professional doors to new opportunities, markets, and collaborations but also opens doors to our higher selves, reconnecting us to those inner riches we may have lost touch with amid the sensory overload of life. Let's go a little further into this journey together, a journey where spirituality, business, and investing converge to change the world for the better.

Some of the actions that you might consider taking include the following:

- Practice active listening and empathy in your daily interactions. Some ways to do this include making active eye contact, pausing before responses, and focusing on your breath.
- Create a personal resilience plan. Build a strong support system of family, friends, or colleagues for emotional and practical assistance. Align your daily actions with your core values and cultivate a positive mindset by focusing on what you can control and reframing negative thoughts. Incorporate healthy lifestyle habits such as regular physical activity, a nutritious diet, and adequate sleep to sustain your energy. Finally, regularly review and update your plan to adapt to new challenges, viewing resilience as a skill that grows stronger with practice.
- Regularly engage in mindfulness practices to cultivate equanimity. Next time you experience a perceived threat or disappointment, challenge yourself to pause and feel that discomfort before you make your next move. Take a deep breath, then assess what you can and cannot control. Try to respond from a space of acceptance and constructive repair rather than from fear and reactivity.
- Reframe negative self-talk to transform your inner critic into an inner ally.
- If you have a spiritual path, pinpoint whether your actions align with your true values and vision. Be honest, and challenge yourself to get back on track. Identify areas where growth requires discomfort and where you might be holding back due to self-doubt.

- Consider working with a coach who can support you in making more intentional decisions.
- Seek out a mentor you admire—an individual who has built a company grounded in spiritual values, driven meaningful impact, and achieved exceptional returns on their investments.

REFLECTION QUESTIONS

- Which old paradigms are you clinging to that may be restricting your expansion?
- What are some ways that you could build more trust within your team at work and with the clients, customers, or members you serve?
- How might you bring the idea of enoughness into your personal and professional lives?
- In reflecting on a period of challenge, are there strategies you have learned from this chapter that you would now apply?
- How might you set a hopeful tone in your engagements with your colleagues?
- What could it look like to engage in your work with an open heart?
- How can you rewrite your self-talk script to infuse more confidence and self-trust into your work and personal lives?

CHAPTER 3

Values and Investing

All profit is not equal. Profit involving shared value enables society to advance and companies to grow faster. Profit at the expense of society is self-defeating.

—**MARK KRAMER**, COFOUNDER OF FSG SOCIAL IMPACT ADVISORS AND A SENIOR FELLOW AT HARVARD KENNEDY SCHOOL

Values are fundamental to organizational culture, employee engagement, investment choices, and stakeholder relationships—in short, just about everything related to business. They guide decision-making, build trust, and set the moral compass for both individuals and organizations. That said, many leaders may not be totally clear on what they value most, let alone how (or even whether) those ethics and ideals inform their leadership choice.

Even if you already strive to lead and invest in an ethical, sustainable way, I find it is always revealing and transformative to revisit, reflect on, and better define your individual and organizational values. Think of it as an inner spiritual mini-retreat, one that helps you establish strategic benchmarks not only for individual development but also in architecting organizational cultures of excellence and impact.

Examples of values that purposeful businesses integrate include honesty, humility, compassion, love, faith, courage, service, acceptance, forgiveness, patience, gratitude, awareness, integrity, and perseverance; essentially, these are guiding values that can promote inner peace and positive action toward others and oneself—often connected to a higher power or sense of meaning beyond the self.

The concept of power in leadership is undergoing a profound transformation, grounded in a shift in values shaping organizational culture. Salesforce research, for example, demonstrates that a sense of purpose in work is one of the top three factors that employees care about.[1] As new tech trends upend old assumptions and patterns, people are rewriting the rules—questioning old hierarchies and setting new professional standards. True power is no longer purely defined through titles and paygrades but rather through trust, alignment with shared purpose, and the ability to inspire meaningful change.

Research consistently shows that leaders who prioritize values-driven empowerment over command-and-control tactics are the ones who cultivate the most resilient, innovative, and collaborative organizations.[2] By earning power through trust and inspiration, these leaders create environments where team members feel valued and motivated to contribute their best ideas. This empowerment fosters continuous learning, adaptability, and a collective commitment to shared goals, enabling organizations to thrive amid disruption and complexity. Such leadership transforms traditional authority into partnership, driving sustained engagement and breakthrough performance. This values-based approach not only engages employees but also fosters a culture where individuals are deeply connected to their work and to the broader causes they care about.

How Does Values-Centered Leadership Translate into Everyday Practice?

The research of Dr. Sarah Soule, a renowned scholar in organizational behavior and social movements and dean of the Stanford Graduate School of Business, provides a compelling lens through which to view the intersection of spirituality, investing, and business. Soule's work emphasizes how collective values, often championed by social movements, can influence corporate behavior and reshape industries. This insight is particularly relevant for those seeking to align their investments and business practices with deeper spiritual or ethical principles.

Soule's studies on corporate social responsibility reveal that, far from being isolated entities, businesses are deeply embedded within societal currents. When investors and consumers demand accountability, transparency, and purpose-driven leadership, companies often respond. These dynamics underscore the power of spiritually aligned investing: not merely to deliver financial returns but to foster systemic change that reflects higher values.

Soule's research offers practical guidance for embedding these principles within organizations. By understanding how movements inspire action and create lasting change, business leaders can design strategies that integrate spiritual values into their operations—whether through ethical supply chains, employee well-being initiatives, or community engagement. In this way, Soule's work bridges the gap between the aspirational ideals of spirituality and the pragmatic realities of modern business.

Her insights remind us that spirituality in business is not a passive ideal but an active force. When collective values are harnessed effectively, they can transform not only individual companies but also entire markets, creating a more just and compassionate economic system.

Rather than leveraging authority to enforce compliance, values-driven leaders build influence through shared purpose and ethical action. This evolution is not just a moral ideal—it's a strategy that will be beneficial to organizations. That is because leaders who engage their teams in cocreating solutions tend to achieve higher performance and satisfaction. For example, according to research conducted by Deloitte, firms with a well-defined mission report a 30 percent increase in innovation rates.[3]

Research consistently shows that businesses driven by purpose and ethical principles significantly outperform their conventional counterparts. A study by the Conscious Capitalism Institute found that conscious businesses—those that integrate purpose and spirituality into their operations—outpaced the S&P 500 by an astonishing 10.5:1 ratio over fifteen years and surpassed even the high-performing "Good-to-Great" companies by 9.3:1 in the same period.[4] Moreover, purpose-oriented companies tend to experience higher productivity and accelerated growth, expanding at three times the rate of their competitors.[5] Ethical leadership further reinforces this advantage, as highly ethical companies have consistently outperformed the S&P 500 by an average of 7.3 percent annually since 2007. These findings highlight the compelling financial case for aligning business with purpose, integrity, and empathy and with a commitment to positive impact.

Why do these values-driven leaders and organizations inspire such trust and loyalty from workers and customers? So much of it has to do with how we define and yield power. Power based on fear or control tends to be both conditional and fleeting, but true earned power creates lasting impact.

The next question is this: *How can leaders build trust and inspire such cooperative, values-based action?*

- **Listen first.** Deep, genuine listening fosters respect and opens pathways to understanding.
- **Encourage collaboration.** Involving others in decisions builds ownership and unlocks innovation.
- **Live your values.** Consistently acting with authenticity cements credibility and trust.

Leaders are not just tasked with achieving results; they're architects of cultures that either enable ongoing progress and growth or obstruct it. This new leadership paradigm invites self-reflection:

- *Are we building trust within our teams, or are we relying on authority and status to achieve outcomes?*
- *How can we align our practices with a shared vision for a sustainable, equitable future?*
- *What organizational voices may not be heard, and how can we elevate those for more inclusive, cooperative decision-making?*

By embracing this shift, leaders move beyond merely managing people and toward empowering them to create organizations that thrive on a shared values-driven purpose as well as on collective success.

Leadership and a Cooperative Vision of Moral Excellence

Establishing a culture rooted in moral and ethical principles can turn leadership into a powerful force for meaningful change. A key component of this paradigm shift involves recognizing and embracing the spiritual aspect of our shared humanity, without compromising business goals. Although the word *spirituality* might evoke discomfort in some professional settings, it need not be taboo in the workplace. Leaders who nurture the moral, ethical, and spiritual capacities of their workforce—fostering integrity, responsibility, and purpose—lay the foundation for resilient and ethical organizations.

This alignment with values and principles also increasingly applies to the investment industry. A deeper purpose, rooted in spiritual principles and ethical values, serves as a compass for decision-making, directing capital toward initiatives that build a more just, sustainable, and harmonious world. In an era when investments wield immense influence on societal and environmental outcomes, aligning investments with a deeper purpose can guide the industry to become a catalyst for meaningful change.

The growth in the global impact investing market demonstrates increasing investor demand for financial returns coupled with measurable social and environmental impact. High-profile investors and funds have illustrated how active engagement and mentorship of portfolio companies can drive positive business outcomes that surpass traditional shareholder primacy approaches. This approach challenges dominant industry patterns that prioritize short-term financial gain and often neglect longer-term social value creation. It's certainly true that overcoming entrenched norms such as shareholder primacy, short holding periods, and narrow risk-return frameworks requires persistent effort to embed principles of humility, trust, and partnership into investment decision-making. However, the potential to redistribute wealth more equitably and to catalyze systemic change makes it a worthwhile pursuit despite these challenges.

At the heart of this transformation lies this question: *What spiritual qualities, values, and principles can create or enhance our culture of moral excellence at work?* Establishing such a culture begins with reflection, for it is in the minds of people that seeds of moral decay and the hope for peace both take root.

By peace, I do not mean that there's no disagreement, but rather that we create brave spaces at work to engage in difficult dialogues. Going beyond the concept of safe spaces, the idea is that no one can really guarantee safety from conflict or disagreement; however, we can acknowledge the courage it takes to speak out and also to hear out your colleagues with openness and grace. Brave spaces are essential in the intersection of spirituality, investing, and business because, rather than seeking the comfort of conformity (or avoidance), they invite participants to engage authentically with vulnerability and courageous dialogue.

In a brave space, individuals are called not only to share their perspectives but also to challenge and be challenged, embracing discomfort as a catalyst for growth and transformation. This environment enables the kind of honest, sometimes tough, conversations that foster greater self-awareness, creativity, and ethical clarity—qualities fundamental to both spiritual practice and principled leadership in business. Rather than insulating from conflict, brave spaces equip business communities to approach complexity, risk, and ambiguity with open minds and grounded confidence—deepening both organizational trust and spiritual integrity.

The golden rule—common to many religious and philosophical traditions—encourages us to treat others as we want to be treated, shifting focus from self-interest to the well-being of others. In the finance and business world, this principle fosters mutual respect and creates the conditions for a culture of peace and moral excellence.

At an organizational level, peace and unity are deeply interconnected. Without peace, unity cannot thrive, and without unity, the long-term success of any business is at risk. Unity dissipates conflict, harmonizes diverse perspectives, and strengthens the collective will to achieve shared goals. Similarly, in investment, a unified vision rooted in shared values allows stakeholders to collaborate more effectively, aligning efforts with the broader purpose of advancing societal progress and environmental stewardship.

The fuel for this unity is shared purpose: a clear, compelling reason for why we show up to work or invest each day, why we strive harder, and why we focus sharper. This purpose must transcend the mere products, services, or financial returns that a business or an investment offers; it should connect to a broader, more inspiring vision of the world we seek to create and the unique role of the organization or investment in contributing to this vision. When every stakeholder—whether an employee, a leader, or an investor—has unshakable clarity of shared purpose, unity becomes a practical foundation for progress, not just an abstract ideal.

As mentioned at the beginning of chapter 1, the international governing council of the Bahá'í Faith, called the Universal House of Justice,[6] released a public letter in 2017 on the vital importance of unity and the prosperity of humanity, noting that every choice we "make as an employee or employer, producer or consumer, borrower or lender, benefactor or beneficiary—leaves a trace, and the moral duty to lead a coherent life demands that one's economic decisions be in accordance with lofty ideals, that the purity of one's aims be matched by the purity of one's actions to fulfil those aims."[7]

This long-term vision for unity is also symbiotic with diversity. Although the term *diversity* often refers to the demographic profiles of employees, customers, or ideas, its definition and reach extend further—to include diversifying income streams, exploring emerging trends, and questioning established practices. Recognizing that current practice is not equal to best practice opens the door for innovation and adaptation. In investment, this perspective enables the industry to respond to evolving societal needs, creating portfolios that reflect resilience, equity, and responsibility.

The principles of purpose, unity, and diversity are interconnected, forming an ecosystem of values that strengthens a culture of moral excellence. To isolate or neglect any of these principles risks undermining the whole. Yet despite the enduring wisdom of ethical values (such as the golden rule), these values are too often acknowledged in concept without translating to widespread action. Where self-interest and a lack of concern for others persist, values-driven work gets siloed—even when collaboration would yield better results. Similarly, investments often prioritize short-term gains over long-term value creation, neglecting the broader impact on society and the planet.

The journey toward moral excellence in leadership, business, and investment demands more than passive acknowledgment of these values. It requires action, integration, and an unwavering commitment to building organizations and investment portfolios that not only thrive financially but also contribute meaningfully to a better, more harmonious world. By embedding a deeper purpose into the core of our decisions, we can ensure that leadership and investment alike serve as guiding lights for a future founded on values and principles that uplift humanity and safeguard our shared home.

Defining Spirituality in Business: Values in Action

Spiritual practices such as meditation, mindful communication, and compassion-based leadership can be more than mere navel-gazing. They can nurture a sense of hope while also transforming it into purposeful action and fostering a more meaningful and dynamic workplace. Such an environment boosts morale and fosters creativity, innovation, and a positive outlook toward future challenges and opportunities.

One example of a company that has integrated spiritual values into corporate action is Innisfree Hotels. By fostering a corporate culture that transcends conventional hospitality norms, Innisfree focuses on creating a work environment that is nurturing, supportive, and spiritually enriching for employees, guests, and stakeholders alike. This approach is evident in their various employee programs that emphasize holistic well-being, encompassing physical, emotional, and spiritual health.

Moreover, Innisfree's commitment to cultural enrichment is reflected in their dedication to local communities and stewardship, aligning with a broader, more inclusive understanding of business success. Their philosophy embodies a belief in the interconnectedness of employee satisfaction, guest experiences, and community well-being, creating a business model that is not just profitable but also spiritually and culturally meaningful. This unique blend of spirituality and cultural investment has become a defining characteristic of Innisfree Hotels, distinguishing them in a competitive industry.

Julian MacQueen, chairman and founder of Innisfree Hotels, shared his perspective on his life's work and the philosophy driving his company's success: "What I am doing is creating a unity of hearts in the workplace," he explained. "Since I'm in the hospitality business, I get paid to serve. Service is such an elevated aspect of my faith. I feel like I've won the lottery. It's amazing that I get paid to do what I'm supposed to do as a spiritual being, a seeker of truth, and a builder of trust."

This vision has guided MacQueen's career for over forty years. He reflected on how he and his wife, Kim, have sought to incorporate psychological principles—concepts they first encountered in the 1970s during their psychology studies—into the workplace in a meaningful way.

"How can the work I do be a spiritual process in serving my employees and society at large?" he mused. "That's what we've been working on at Innisfree Hotels—and it seems to be working," he added, noting that this has manifested itself in high employee retention and strong economic growth.

At Innisfree Hotels, the MacQueens have implemented what they call the cooperative mode,[8] designed to ensure ethical interpersonal interactions based on values and virtues. One key element of this approach is recognizing and addressing power plays—behaviors people use, consciously or unconsciously, to manipulate others.

"Power plays can manifest in many ways," MacQueen noted. "For instance, someone might come into a room speaking loudly, asserting themselves to intimidate. That's a power play." MacQueen emphasized that awareness is key. By training employees to recognize these ingrained behaviors and understand both their origins and their impact, Innisfree Hotels creates a culture where such tactics do not have a place.

"When we recognize power plays, we can talk about them, clean them up, and ensure our interactions reflect our highest qualities—both personally and professionally," he explained.

One of the challenges Innisfree Hotels faced was scaling this values-driven approach across a diverse workforce of sixteen hundred to two thousand employees, spread across twenty-eight hotels and thirteen restaurants. Their employees range from highly paid executives with advanced degrees to housekeepers and dishwashers, making up about 85 percent of the workforce.

"To make this work, we had to keep it simple," MacQueen said. "These tools are accessible to everyone, regardless of their role or background."

Cooperative mode tools are practical principles designed to foster trust, accountability, and authentic collaboration across the organization. They involve the following guidelines:

- **No power plays:** Avoiding attempts to impose one's will on others, honoring individual readiness and willingness.
- **No rescues:** Encouraging personal growth by refraining from doing tasks for others that they can perform themselves.
- **No secrets or lies:** Committing to transparency by avoiding secrecy, dishonesty, or withholding important information, which can erode trust.
- **Being accountable:** Taking full ownership of one's mistakes and taking proactive steps to resolve issues and learn from experience.
- **Inclusion:** Intentionally fostering an environment where every person belongs and is heard.
- **Checking out paranoid fantasies:** Directly addressing suspicions or doubts with individuals or groups to reduce misunderstandings.
- **Sharing a resentment:** Encouraging the open communication of negative feelings, allowing for healing and restoration of trust.
- **Confidentiality:** Respecting privacy by keeping personal or sensitive information protected unless permission is granted to share.

Together, these principles create a foundational framework that aligns business practices with spiritual values such as integrity, respect, and mutual care—an approach that nurtures both individual growth and organizational health.

By providing employees with these tools, Innisfree Hotels seeks to foster an environment full of brave spaces where individuals can bring their genuine, true selves to work each day. "We're not psychologists," MacQueen clarified. "We're just equipping people with practical tools to build clean, authentic relationships in their personal and professional lives. When everyone feels free to be who they truly are, they perform at their best, and the organization thrives."

The MacQueens' goal is to ensure that this approach is replicable across all levels of the organization and its locations. "We've created a strategy that can be scaled and built upon," he explained. "The simplicity of these tools is what makes them effective. They're not just theoretical—they're actionable. And by applying them consistently, we're seeing the benefits in the workplace and beyond."

Through their innovative approach, the MacQueens demonstrate how integrating spirituality, ethical principles, and practical tools can transform a business and the lives of those within it. Their journey offers a blueprint for creating a culture of service, trust, and authenticity in any organization—an inspiring reminder of the profound impact that values-driven leadership can have on both business success and the human spirit.

The intersection of spirituality and business, underpinned by a culture of hope and transformation, is not only beneficial but also essential in today's rapidly evolving business landscape. As leaders, founders, and investors, we have an opportunity for increased engagement around spiritual principles in people's professional journeys, thereby contributing to a more humane, compassionate, and hopeful business world.

Leading with Values: The Story of Douglas Henck

Another corporate pioneer successfully integrating spirituality into his management style and practice is Douglas Henck. Henck's insurance career spans over forty-five years, during which he worked with multinational corporations, managed operations in more than ten countries across Asia, and held responsibility for tens of thousands of employees. Beginning his career as an actuary and a financial officer, Henck later transitioned into strategic management, driven by a fascination with the concept of workplace motivation.

Throughout his career, Henck regularly asked himself, *What motivates people to go to work and work hard?* His exploration of this question led him to an enduring truth: People are most inspired when they believe they're part of something that makes a difference. For Henck, facilitating this sense of purpose became the cornerstone of his leadership philosophy.

Henck's approach to leadership is deeply influenced by the Bahá'í concept of unity in diversity, which helped him understand and balance the needs of diverse stakeholders. He developed a framework emphasizing fairness, shared purpose, and ethical action:

- First, consider all stakeholders, not just those with deep pockets or important titles.
- Second, work to foster unity among these diverse stakeholders.
- Third, balance their needs equitably.

At a time when such principles were considered unconventional, Henck used them to design fair and effective insurance products, implement compliance measures, and ensure that no stakeholder took more than their fair share. Through decades of experience, Henck demonstrated that leading with values is not just a moral imperative—it's the foundation of long-term success for individuals, organizations, and society.

Business Justice: Aligning Values with Impact

For yet another example of a notable leader incorporating spiritual values into business, we return to Daryn Dodson, the managing partner of Illumen Capital and Ben & Jerry's board member we met in chapter 2.

Dodson describes the concept of spiritual capital as an inner asset comprising values, ethics, and a sense of purpose, one that guides decision-making in contexts ranging from team meetings to boardrooms. He shared his vision of a values-driven company through the lens of his work on the Ben & Jerry's board. Central to his perspective is another concept he developed called business justice.

Business justice, as Dodson explained, "is the idea that a company can rise to meet the challenges of its time by grounding itself in values and aligning with those values in a way that drives innovation and transforms the world." He pointed to Ben & Jerry's as a prime example of a company embodying this ethos, with its three-part mission: social, economic, and product quality. This holistic vision aims to build the best ice cream company in the world while also creating meaningful social and environmental change.

A symbol of Ben & Jerry's commitment to business justice can be found in its Flavor Graveyard, a unique attraction at their Vermont ice cream factory where visitors can peruse poetic and often humorous headstones for discontinued ice cream flavors. For Dodson, this graveyard serves as a metaphor for the company's relentless pursuit of innovation across its three missions.

"The Flavor Graveyard reminds us that businesses must continuously innovate," he said. "It's about pushing forward important, values-driven concepts that honor the company's founding principles—such as peace, environmental sustainability, and transparency."

This playful practice celebrates the company's many flavor experimentations and collaborations, sometimes around shared causes with other companies. One example of a discontinued favor is Fossil Fuel, an iced sweet cream with chocolate cookie pieces, fudge dinosaurs, and a fudge swirl. The choice to retire this flavor poetically represented the company's view that fossil fuels are better in the ground.[9]

Dodson highlighted several other examples of how Ben & Jerry's operationalizes its values. The company has long championed environmental sustainability through its packaging and product innovations. Its commitment to transparency led it to eliminate genetically modified organisms from ingredient lists across all its products, ensuring that customers know exactly what they're consuming. These efforts reflect a deeper ethos, where the principles of business justice guide every decision.

"For a company to embody business justice, it must see itself as a steward of societal improvement—not as an externality or as a side project but as the very driving force of its business," Dodson emphasized. At Ben & Jerry's, this ethos cultivates a high level of trust and affinity among its fans who admire the brand's authenticity and steadfast commitment to purpose. By pursuing this strategy, Ben & Jerry's has also achieved over forty years of business success, solidifying its position as an iconic brand that actively integrates social responsibility with profitability.

Ultimately, Dodson's vision for business justice challenges companies to go beyond profit and to consider their role in shaping a more equitable and sustainable world. By rooting their missions in values and aligning their actions with those values, companies can build trust, inspire loyalty, and drive transformative change—demonstrating that justice in business is not only possible but also essential.

Divest–Invest Philanthropy

In 2013, I had the opportunity to join the Ben and Jerry's Foundation board on a visit to New Orleans's Cancer Alley, the local nickname given to a stretch of the Mississippi River dominated by more than two hundred petrochemical plants and refineries. There we met a group called the Louisiana Bucket Brigade, an environmental health and justice organization.

The Louisiana Bucket Brigade shared their optimism and excitement about foundations shifting capital from fossil fuels into impact-oriented solutions. They explained that this trend added greater momentum to their work, which involves partnering with communities close to industrial sites to map the contamination of their air quality and build cases to address this. Discovering that they were part of a global movement of impact investors and renewable energy solutions gave them not only something to fight against but also something to advocate for.

This encouraged and inspired me at a time when I was helping to grow and manage the Divest-Invest Philanthropy initiative, a coalition of more than 170 foundations representing over $50 billion in assets under management. In particular, our work focused on shifting capital from fossil fuels into impact-oriented solutions.

One of the foundations that joined this coalition was the Rockefeller Brothers Fund. Descendants of John Rockefeller spoke about how their famous ancestor had made his fortune by pioneering a new form of energy through oil during his time. They noted that if he were alive today, it is very likely this forward-thinking leader would be at the forefront of the new innovation curve: pioneering renewable energy. In this spirit, his family, alongside many others, chose to move their assets away from the fossil fuel industry, aligning with the values of innovation and progress that defined Rockefeller's legacy.

This narrative underscores the importance of alignment at the individual, organizational, and societal levels. It reflects a commitment to ensuring that our actions and investments are not only financially sound but also ethically and morally grounded. By embracing this holistic approach, we can contribute to the creation of a more just, sustainable, and flourishing world for all.

Bahá'u'lláh, founder of the Bahá'í Faith, called on humanity to "be generous in prosperity . . . Be a treasure to the poor, an admonisher to the rich, an answerer of the cry of the needy."[10] This statement serves as a powerful directive for living a life aligned with the needs of society. It underscores the importance of daily practices that keep us attuned to societal needs and cognizant of the expansive impact of our actions, as echoed in seventeenth-century English poet John Donne's famous assertion that no man is an island, but part of the main.[11]

In its March 2017 message, the Bahá'í Faith's Universal House of Justice further clarified the challenges of viewing wealth solely in terms of accumulation and consumption: "To view the worth of an individual chiefly in terms of how much one can accumulate and how many goods one can consume relative to others is wholly alien to Bahá'í thought . . . Wealth must serve humanity. Its use must accord with spiritual principles; systems must be created in their light."[12]

When I founded Impact Experience, it was as a testament to these ideals, aiming to build inclusive societies and foster communities that embody consultation and the principle that wealth must serve humanity. This initiative has united over fifty-five hundred individuals across more than thirty communities, emphasizing bridge-building and community enhancement.

At Impact Experience, we prioritize genuine connection by investing deeply in relationships with community members and partners—getting to know their families, stories, and lives beyond the surface. This proactive approach builds trust and lays a strong foundation for meaningful collaboration while minimizing potential conflicts.

This approach also manifests itself through the investing and acquisition work I engage in through my firm LightPost Capital. For both of these initiatives (and indeed, in every venture I undertake) the guiding question is this: *How can we infuse spiritual values into the fabric of the culture so that everyone has the opportunity to thrive?* This answer will vary depending on organizational values and goals.

To develop a culture of excellence, a whole host of factors are needed. Let's start with one we've already touched on: the notion of trust. Overwhelming field evidence, research-based studies from countless scholars, and case study after case study all show that trust is one of the foundational pillars in an organization. It's one key factor that can change everything, serving as the glue that holds it all together. Trust speeds up responsible decision-making, problem-solving, conflict management, and strategic planning. It develops character, integrity, leadership, and lasting personal and professional relationships.

As leaders, we sometimes lack the practical know-how by which we can consistently operationalize seemingly simple yet very complex and profound concepts such as ethics and integrity into our organizations. Trust can lay the foundation on which to build other core competencies that can develop a sustained competitive advantage through a culture of excellence. In particular, it helps deepen collaboration and commitment to shared values rather than siloing or even competitive infighting.

In terms of operationalizing trust-based ethics, it helps to build more bridges and get people talking. For example, through Impact Experience, we have brought together the investment and grant-making teams from foundations that do not often, if ever, get the opportunity to spend quality time together and collaborate. Through immersive experiences, they have the opportunity to align relationships and goals with mission. Given that most foundations across the industry experience this disconnect between their investments and grant-making teams, this kind of intentional connection is rare. Reflective practice is central to this process, encouraging leaders and team members alike to examine the impact of our actions and ensure that they align with our values of ethical business. At Impact Experience, we go beyond just talk to focus on action-oriented engagement, translating principles into tangible outcomes that benefit not only our organization but also society at large. By embodying the change we seek, we create ripples of transformation that guide businesses toward equitable and inclusive practices, honoring our shared humanity and shaping a better future.

Strategy for Values-Aligned Investing

Developing a values-aligned approach to investing is an ongoing process. It involves exploring conscious investment strategies that help ensure that financial and societal objectives can be holistically, sustainably achieved. This means formulating key values, exploring various investing approaches, setting financial and impact goals, and customizing a portfolio in harmony with an individual's or a group's beliefs.

The process begins with a deep understanding of core values and priorities. It challenges us to identify causes to support as well as industries and practices to avoid. An investor might, for example, focus on sustainability and community development while shifting capital away from fossil fuels and private prisons. This reflection on values can take place at the individual, organization, and family levels.

Aligning values with financial objectives also requires ample research to explore different investment strategies. These might include the following:

- **Positive screening:** Selecting companies or initiatives consistent with certain ethical values and societal goals (e.g., clean energy or gender equity).
- **Negative screening:** In this strategy, investors exclude certain companies or industries from their portfolios based on specific ethical, social, or environmental criteria that do not align with their values or investment goals.
- **Shareholder advocacy:** This is when investors use their rights as company owners to influence corporate policies and practices on issues such as governance, social responsibility, and environmental impact, often through proposals, proxy votes, and dialogue with management.

Set Financial and Impact Objectives

Striking the right balance between impactful change and financial returns is key. This applies to all investments, from long-term wealth-building for 401(k) retirement and legacy planning to small onetime savings targets. I have worked closely with financial institutions, advisers, and individual investors focused on designing portfolios that reflect core values, foster a sense of purpose, and contribute to a more equitable and sustainable world while still achieving financial success.

One company praised for its values-driven organizational and investment strategy is Salesforce. Under the leadership of Marc Benioff, Salesforce has demonstrated a profound commitment to integrating ethical values into its business. Benioff, a proponent of the concept of compassionate capitalism, often credits his leadership approach to spiritual teachings and mindfulness practices that influence how he builds and guides the company. He has spoken extensively about the importance of leading with purpose and aligning business goals with a greater sense of service to humanity and the planet, as reflected in his book *Trailblazer: The Power of Business as the Greatest Platform for Change.*[13]

This spiritual ethos is evident in Salesforce's integration of sustainability as a core company value, alongside trust, customer success, innovation, and equality. The company has set a commitment around net zero emissions across its value chain, which includes operating on 100 percent renewable energy and embedding environmental, social, and governance goals into executive compensation to ensure accountability and progress. Benioff's leadership philosophy and practice emphasize that companies have both the power and the responsibility to drive meaningful change in the world. His approach exemplifies how purpose-driven leadership can inspire transformative impact while fostering long-term success.[14]

Regenerating Consciousness and Capital

The intersection of spirituality and business emphasizes the idea of regenerating consciousness and capital. By drawing on spiritual principles during investments and decision-making, leaders can build trust and accountability among consumers, employees, and stakeholders. This helps to elevate and transform both our worldviews and our wealth into something truly regenerative for the world.

One of the guiding principles in my career as an investor has been the belief that wealth should be used to benefit all humanity. Leaders have the ability to aim their decision-making toward concern for the common good. There is an opportunity to engage meditative practices and weave principles of love, integrity, and interdependence into investment paradigms and organizational fabrics so that business ventures appeal not only to financial gain but also to spiritual pursuits.

Wayne Silby, founder of the $45 billion investment management company Calvert Funds, credits his holistic leadership style in part to personal spiritual practices, such as float tanks and mindfulness meditation grounded in Eastern spiritual practices. These disciplines help Silby achieve clarity and purpose in decision-making.

Over the years, when faced with thorny problems and foundational business decisions, Silby has relied on a go-to modality that he says guides him to new epiphanies and innovative solutions: spending time in a float tank. He credits his float tank meditations with helping him engage creatively with competitors and develop viable pathways forward. This demonstrates the power of quieting mental noise to foster creativity and strategic thinking. According to Silby, integrating spiritual tools and practices, such as meditation, into the decision-making processes enhances focus and compassion, drives innovation, and promotes both transformative leadership and long-term success across industries.

For Daryn Dodson of Illumen Capital, one of the best spiritual practices involves getting outside at dawn with a fishing pole. Fishing is far more than a hobby for him. In Dodson's experience, it's a form of meditation that fosters reflection, awe, and connection to the natural world. He recalls that, since childhood, he has viewed fishing as a spiritual endeavor, marveling at the vastness of nature and the interconnectedness of life. Observing phenomena such as migratory fish returning to their birthplace inspires him to embrace the importance of pausing, returning to one's roots, and maintaining a sense of wonder—essential elements for innovation and thoughtful leadership. This practice allows him to slow down, clear his mind, and approach his work with clarity and purpose.

It also helps to ground his investment career and decision-making. He has often found that, during or after a fishing trip, he gains sudden insights into improving investment strategies, not because fishing is goal-oriented but because it reconnects him with the human experience of being present. This fosters deeper receptivity and creativity in both business and community.

According to Dodson, "The ability to be fully present, to genuinely and clearly listen to colleagues from a place of love and joy, and to remain open to being transformed by what others are saying is, in my view, incredibly important and often lacking in the world of corporate investing."

In addition to my interviews with Silby and Dodson, I had the chance to speak with Dr. Ashby Monk, the executive and research director of the Stanford Research Initiative on Long-Term Investing. During our conversation, Monk shared his mission to inspire the next generation of investors.

"There are millions of students out there," he explained, "and I want them to know they can build investment careers within organizations that have an incredible positive mission behind them." Drawing from over twenty years of experience studying and advising investment organizations, Monk emphasized how purpose-driven work can align with financial success.

One unique aspect of Monk's approach to leadership and decision-making is his incorporation of mindfulness. Monk uses mindfulness as a tool for uncovering and addressing negative behavioral patterns in the finance world. For him, mindfulness is not just about formal breathwork or meditation separate from everyday life; it's about creating moments of intentional reflection every day, including at work.

"I like the idea of having a mindfulness moment at the beginning of any key decision-making," he shared. "You can create that synthetically by starting a meeting with a moment of reflection." Walking meetings, he noted, are a particular favorite of his. "Walking puts the problems in front of us and allows for silence and thoughtfulness. We don't have to fill every moment with talking, and stepping away from devices makes the experience even more productive."

Monk's insights reflect a deeply practical approach to integrating mindfulness into the high-pressure world of finance. His methods highlight how thoughtful pauses and deliberate practices can lead to more effective and ethical investment decisions. Monk even cowrote a paper on the rise of mindfulness and its integration into financial decision-making, "De-Biasing Investment Decisions: The Role of Mindfulness,"[15] in which he explores how mindfulness can help investors overcome cognitive biases.

In 1995, the investing legend and philanthropist Charlie Munger delivered a talk at Harvard University, "The Psychology of Human Misjudgment," where he said, "I came to the psychology of human misjudgment almost against my will; I rejected it until I realized that my attitude was costing me a lot of money, and it reduced my ability to help everything I loved."[16]

Charlie Munger's candid admission reveals the profound impact of psychological biases on decision-making, even for seasoned investors. His reluctant journey into understanding human misjudgment highlights the transformative power of reflection and self-awareness in both financial success and personal growth. By acknowledging and overcoming his initial resistance, Munger not only enhanced his investment acumen but also expanded his capacity to contribute meaningfully to his passions.

Integrating values into investing and business decision-making is not merely some aspirational pipe dream. Rather, it's a crucial element in developing a just, sustainable, and flourishing world. Spirituality, belonging, and ethical practice all empower individuals and organizations to lead with purpose and help transform society.

How can we move from theory and good intentions toward more practical—and profitable—values-based investments and business decisions?

The answer, lives within. Begin by listening closely—to the quiet pulse of your own values and how they call you to act in the world. Let your business goals take root there, nourished by integrity. And as you move forward, seek companions whose visions are aligned with your own, so that together you can engage in investments and endeavors that promote shared flourishing.

REFLECTION QUESTIONS

- Are you doing the inner work to consider the ways that your values show up in different aspects of your life?
- What impact would you like to see in the world as a result of the work you do? In addition, what causes and/or aspects of society do you wish to align with, influence, or support?
- Are there any larger-scale responsible investment or business events you can attend and engage with? If so, what key topics, goals, or values can you explore or promote related to societal empowerment? How can you expand possibilities for community engagement and collaboration to help amplify innovative responsible trends?
- What conditions must be present to nurture a culture of moral excellence at work?
- What core spiritual qualities are relevant to your work or business?
- How can you fully operationalize ethics and responsibility through the products or services you offer as well as within the organization as a whole?

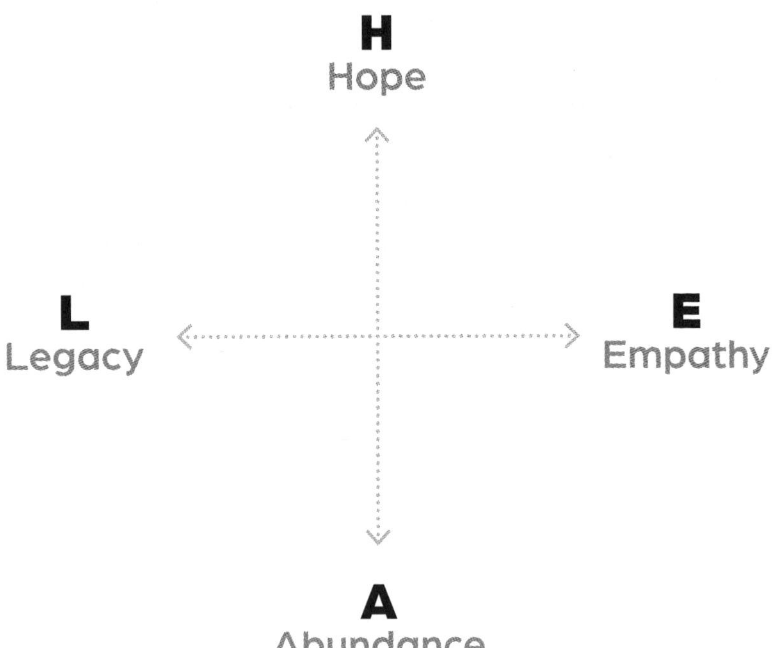
H
Hope
L
Legacy
E
Empathy
A
Abundance

PART 2

THE HEAL—HOPE, EMPATHY, ABUNDANCE, AND LEGACY—FRAMEWORK

CHAPTER 4

Hope: Power of Resiliency

Hope is often misunderstood. People tend to think that it is simply passive wishful thinking: "I hope something will happen but I'm not going to do anything about it." This is indeed the opposite of real hope, which requires action and engagement.

—**DR. JANE GOODALL,** PROMINENT ZOOLOGIST, PRIMATOLOGIST, AND ANTHROPOLOGIST

A few years ago, while reflecting on the COVID-19 pandemic, a good friend said aloud, "I wonder what your mother would make of this situation and what her guidance would be for us all."

This was no casual inquiry. The question cut to the core of something I had been reflecting on for years. My mother passed away and transitioned to the next world several years ago, yet her wisdom remains a guiding force in my life. Over time, I have realized that one of the key ways that my mother processed the world comes down to this: finding hope and light even in the darkest of times.

The question resurfaced amid more recent conversations about humanity's ability to build something new and better in the aftermath of the COVID-19 crisis. The pandemic laid bare the fragility of our systems and the inequities embedded within them. Yet, in the rubble of what was, I am sure my mother would have recognized and nurtured the undeniable yearning for something greater—a belief that we can reshape our world. It is in this hope, as fragile as it sometimes feels, that the seeds of transformation lie.

Now that we have laid the groundwork for understanding the profound intersection of spirituality, investing, and business, it is time to plant some practical, and transformational, seeds. The second part of this book will help us intentionally weave these realms together through the HEAL framework of hope, empathy, abundance, and legacy. Think of these as tools for cultivating a more conscientious and holistic approach to financial decisions and business practices. Each one uncovers actionable strategies for aligning your financial and business goals with your deepest values. From that alignment, we can help grow a more equitable, sustainable, and spiritually enriched world, one grounded in connection.

Looking back, I often know what my mother would make of any situation and what her guidance would be. The answers are one and the same: Find the hope and light it up. Focus on the next positive thing. Make that seed grow.

A Legacy of Hope

One of my mother's gifts that I value most was her introduction to the Bahá'í Faith during my formative years. Through its teachings, I found both a framework for understanding the world and a reservoir of hope to draw on during life's most challenging moments. The Bahá'í writings speak of the time we are living through as a transitional moment, one marked by both upheaval and renewal.

Shoghi Effendi, the Guardian of the Bahá'í Faith, described it poignantly: "We stand on the threshold of an age whose convulsions proclaim alike the death-pangs of the old order and the birth-pangs of the new."[1]

This resonates deeply with the state of the world today. The old paradigms—rooted in exploitation, division, and short-term thinking—are faltering under their own weight. Yet, amid this collapse, an undeniable energy of renewal is growing, budding, preparing to bloom. People are coming together to reimagine what is possible—in business, in professions, in investment, and in personal lives.

The year I am writing this, 2025, began with numerous challenges: from the devastating wildfires in Los Angeles to the persistent political and social upheaval across the globe. In a world brimming with adversity, how do we resist falling into paralyzing uncertainty and despair? How do we instead cultivate and sustain hope? More crucially, how do we channel hope into action, harnessing its transformative power to create meaningful change?

In this chapter, we delve into this first element of the HEAL framework. Hope acts as a catalyst for innovation and resilience, empowering leaders and organizations to navigate complexity with a forward-looking mindset. Leaders who intentionally integrate spiritual principles and practices into their work environments often foster cultures of transformation and optimism. When these elements of hope inform strategy, decision-making, and collaboration in business and investing, incredible things can happen.

At its core, this chapter highlights how spirituality and hope work in tandem to drive progress in business. Hope can go far beyond mere sentiment to become a strategic asset—a guiding principle that encourages individuals and organizations to aspire toward a more humane, compassionate, and purpose-driven future.

By embracing spiritual principles, professionals can contribute to creating a business world where hope and transformation are not only possible but also integral to success.

Let's explore hope as a guiding principle—a beacon that can inspire us to work collectively toward a better world. We'll delve into practical and meaningful steps that each of us can take to nurture hope in our daily lives and professional endeavors.

Through this exploration, you are invited to do the following:

- Discover the true meaning of hope.
- Reflect on what hope means for you as a leader, both in your professional and in your personal lives.

Hope is deeply intertwined with uncertainty, particularly in these times, and with our ability to shape the future. This challenges us to embrace hope not only as a source of resilience but also as an active force for transformation in the face of challenges.

The Active Cultivation of Hope

The word *hope* suggests a sense of trust and optimism about future outcomes. It's both emotional and cognitive, encompassing the desire for a particular outcome as well as the belief in the possibility of that outcome. The etymology traces back to the Old English word *hopa*, related to the verb *hopian*, which meant "to wish for something with expectation of its fulfillment."

When looking at the state of the world today, cultivating hope might seem like a daunting task. According to the UK think tank Resolution Foundation, 34 percent of British people aged eighteen to twenty-four reported symptoms of mental health issues such as depression or anxiety in 2021 and 2022, up from 24 percent in 2000.[2]

Similarly, Champion Health's survey of over four thousand workers in the UK and Europe revealed that 40 percent of those aged sixteen to twenty-four show clinically relevant anxiety symptoms.

It's not just young workers who are struggling. Champion Health also found that 53 percent of all employees feel down, depressed, or hopeless, and 38 percent report workplace stress, with financial worries as the leading external stressor.[3] Gallup's January 2025 data show that indicators of employee engagement in the US have fallen to just 31 percent in 2024, its lowest in a decade.[4] This decline translates to about 8 million fewer engaged workers since 2020, including a drop of 3.2 million in 2023 alone.[5]

Amid such discouraging data, the active cultivation of hope becomes essential. To counter these challenges and foster resilience, we must lead and model hope as a powerful practice that demands daily effort at both the individual and the organizational levels. Although the gloom and doom can seem overpowering at times, you would be surprised by how much a team can withstand and grow if they practice fostering hope, belonging, and resilience. These elements can help create a thriving supportive work environment that serves as a buffer against burnout and job stress.

Coherence ensures that all parts of the system work synergistically, reinforcing a clear sense of purpose and direction. By promoting coherence, organizations sustain hope and create environments where meaningful, shared progress feels attainable.

A study published by meQuilibrium, a digital platform and app focused on workforce resilience, highlights just how powerful hope can be in the workplace. In their study, they define hope as a combination of optimism and self-efficacy. The study, which surveyed nearly six thousand adults, found that employees with high levels of hope are 74 percent less likely to experience burnout, anxiety, or depression.[6] They are also 33 percent less likely to engage in quiet quitting and are almost half (49 percent less) as likely to consider leaving their jobs, compared to their less hopeful counterparts. Dr. Brad Smith, meQuilibrium's chief science officer, explains that hope is built on resilience, which comes from qualities such as positivity, confidence, and problem-solving.

When organizations focus on these traits, employees naturally feel more motivated and engaged. Managers play a big part in this—supportive managers make employees feel valued and respected, while we have likely all experienced the kind of atmosphere that ensues with unsupportive leaders. In short, investing in hope and resilience leads to happier, stronger teams.[7]

One distinguished leader who actively cultivates hope in business is Shiva Dustdar, director of the European Investment Bank Institute and the first woman to lead this pivotal institution. An advocate for innovation and sustainable finance, Dustdar has dedicated her career to understanding how we can better function as individuals and as societies.

I had the opportunity to speak to Dustdar about the transformative power of cultivating hope at work as well as some practical strategies she uses to foster these qualities in a professional environment. Being raised a Bahá'í, she began by picking up a book and drawing my attention to one of her favorite quotations from 'Abdu'l-Bahá, the eldest son of Bahá'u'lláh and a renowned ambassador for international peace and social justice:

> I desire distinction for you . . . But this distinction must not depend upon wealth—that they should become more affluent than other people. I do not desire for you financial distinction. It is not an ordinary distinction I desire; not scientific, commercial, industrial distinction. For you I desire spiritual distinction—that is, you must become

> eminent and distinguished in morals . . . You must become distinguished for loving humanity, for unity and accord, for love and justice. In brief, you must become distinguished in all the virtues of the human world—for faithfulness and sincerity, for justice and fidelity, for firmness and steadfastness, for philanthropic deeds and service to the human world, for love toward every human being, for unity and accord with all people, for removing prejudices and promoting international peace . . . I desire this distinction for you. This must be the point of distinction among you.[8]

"This quotation," she said, "is what allows me to be more present in the moment and more conscious of my decisions when it comes to investing." For Dustdar, recalling the stated hopes of 'Abdu'l-Bahá keeps her grounded in her own vision of the future world she wants her choices and her capital to nurture.

Dustdar also highlighted Gandhi's words: "Your thoughts become your words, your words become your actions, your actions become your habits, your habits become your values, your values become your destiny."

Our individual and collective destiny is shaped by the sum of our thoughts and beliefs, which Dustdar seeks to intentionally redirect with the help of community, prayer, meditation, and action. But above all, she said, hope comes from within. Dustdar likened the cultivation of hope to the airplane oxygen mask analogy—taking care of your own positivity first so that you can better support others.

Once you can learn to consciously redirect your thoughts and ground in the moment, optimism can become a powerful, even a transformational, lens. Dustdar's final reference in our conversation was to Winston Churchill's insight: "A pessimist sees the difficulty in every opportunity; an optimist sees the opportunity in every difficulty." If you can train your mind to reflexively find opportunities in crises, your leadership can find the hope and light it up.

Dustdar supports her own mental hope training by engaging with networks and communities, including social media and chat groups of like-minded individuals who share her values and who actively encourage hope and mutual support. Through these practices, Dustdar has built a resilient foundation of hope and positivity in her life and work.

This exchange with Dustdar led me to consider what other steps leaders can take to cultivate hope. One article, by *Forbes*, recommends actively and genuinely listening to your team, nurturing a sense of shared meaning, and leading by example.[9] When I read that article, it immediately brought to mind May Samali.

Samali is the founder and CEO of the Human Leadership Lab, a global leadership development company. As a speaker, facilitator, coach, researcher, investor, and board director, she wears many hats to unlock leadership potential in organizations, teams, and individuals. She highlighted the importance of practicing hope as a deliberate, ongoing effort.

"It's about being the change you want to see in the world," she said, acknowledging that this is no easy task and often requires going against the grain. Here are a few ways that Samali embodies her hope through action:

- **Ground yourself.** Staying grounded starts with personal practices such as connecting with nature, prayer, meditation, or gratitude—activities that build resilience, strength, and courage to lead with optimism, as discussed in Chapter 2.

- **Speak truth.** Samali champions values such as justice, compassion, and bravery, even when faced with resistance or uncertainty.
- **Experiment.** Leadership, Samali explained, is a skill honed through practice and trial and error, not perfection. By adopting an experimental mindset, leaders can remain open to new possibilities, fostering a sense of abundance and believing that solutions and victories are achievable, even in the face of adversity.
- **Connect.** Crucially, hope is not a solitary journey. Building an aligned community of allies and supporters provides both practical guidance and emotional sustenance, creating a network that helps sustain optimism in action.

By integrating these strategies, leaders can create a resilient workforce ready to navigate uncertainty and achieve success.

Hope as a Lifeline

It's always interesting to me how so many people have a negative view of the concept of optimism. I have always subscribed to the perspective that optimists get things done. That is because I've always found power in realistic optimism. I often think about the quotation from Martin Luther King, Jr.: "We must accept finite disappointment, but never lose infinite hope."

I had the privilege of interviewing my dear friend and mentor, Marshall Ganz, a renowned professor at Harvard Kennedy School and an architect behind many global organizing movements. Ganz's insights on hope, spirituality, and leadership have profoundly shaped how I understand and approach these topics.

As he shared with me, "Hope is the belief in the probability of the possible rather than the necessity of the probable." This philosophy underpins his groundbreaking work on public narrative, which emphasizes the power of storytelling through the story of self, the story of us, and the story of now.

Professor Ganz's reflections remind me of the ancient questions he often draws on from Rabbi Hillel, a Jewish religious leader and one of the best known historical Jewish sages. Hillel taught the importance of self-awareness, ethical responsibility, and timely action. He framed these ideas through guiding questions, such as "If I am not for myself, who will be for me? When I am for myself alone, what am I? If not now, when?"[10]

These musings reflect a balance between self-care and care for others, highlighting the interconnectedness of individual growth and contribution to the collective well-being. They encourage proactive, compassionate engagement with the world, underscoring the idea that hope is not passive but active.

Ganz describes hope as a blend of courage, love, and a leap of faith toward creating meaningful experiences for ourselves and others. As he put it, "It's not just a wish but an experience."

He cultivates and shares this experience of hope through small tangible actions that inspire a belief in possibility and transcendence. To integrate spirituality into business, he recommends fostering this kind of action-driven hope—one that motivates us to persevere, innovate, and connect. Practices such as mindful communication, meditation, and compassion-based leadership all serve to transform hope from a fleeting feeling into purposeful, integrated action, creating environments that are not only productive but also deeply meaningful. Although hope emerges as an inner resource, rooted in recognizing our value, it also draws on our shared humanity and the transformative power of love and community.

Imagine a hope-driven CEO of a small tech start-up facing unprecedented challenges during a turbulent economic period. As the company struggles with dwindling resources and growing uncertainty, the leader grounded in hope knows it is still possible to shift the narrative. Instead of focusing on the difficulties, she encourages the team to share their personal stories—why they joined the company, what they valued most about their work, and the impact they hoped to create. Through these conversations, employees rediscover that spirit of shared purpose, commitment, and excitement for the future.

She goes further to introduce weekly mindfulness sessions and small team-driven initiatives to tackle immediate problems. As mindsets shift back toward the positive, it becomes easier to focus—and get creative about impact and problem-solving. One team develops a more sustainable, efficient approach to resource allocation, saving the company thousands of dollars. Another finds a creative way to pivot their product to meet a growing market need.

This hypothetical is not just theory. It well describes dark periods experienced by many of the CEOs and founders I have interviewed for this book. As leaders, when we lean into sincere, strategic hope, we can cause a cultural shift, transforming a bleak situation into a story of resilience, collaboration, and renewed belief in a shared mission.

As Ganz put it, "Hope is the commitment leap. It takes courage, love, and a belief in the possibility of what can be—and when nurtured, it can inspire transformation at every level."

Fostering Hope in the Workplace

Todd Khozein is cofounder and CEO of SecondMuse, an impact-driven innovation company that has touched communities around the world. SecondMuse fosters resilient economies by empowering entrepreneurs and cultivating ecosystems that prioritize inclusivity, dignity, and environmental health.

In our conversation, we explored the concept of hope in the workplace, and Khozein shared profound insights into how leaders can instill hope within their teams while fostering a culture of mutual care and shared purpose.

His first insight involved the idea of hope through mutual commitment. Khozein emphasized that the traditional employer-employee relationship often revolves around self-interest and transactional interactions exemplified by a phrase often reduced to the acronym WIIFM: "What's in it for me?" However, he advocates for a new paradigm—one where employers and employees actively look out for one another. This requires explicit agreements and a shared mindset and vision. Imbalance can lead to injustice; however, with cooperation and reciprocity, optimism and hope can thrive.

For true reciprocity, leaders should involve their teams in shaping the future. By fostering open dialogue and identifying shared goals, organizations cultivate cooperation, collective ownership, and purpose. This requires strong connections and compassionate conflict management. At the core of effective leadership is a focus on relationships. Khozein stressed that everything—policies, communication, and decision-making—must prioritize fairness, care, and respect.

Second, he encourages those he works with to rethink their assumptions about human nature. Khozein highlighted that fostering hope begins with a shift in core beliefs about oneself and others. Too often, our society views human nature through a negative lens, assuming self-interest and competition. Yet Khozein argued that when properly nurtured and supported, human nature is instead inherently noble—and leaders can tap into this potential by creating systems that reflect this belief.

Before making decisions, leaders can check in with themselves to determine whether their assumptions lean toward their higher or lower nature. If we look at famous political philosophers, we can see that the range of core beliefs on this topic has historically varied wildly. Thomas Hobbes famously described human life in its natural state as nasty, brutish, and short, a phrase originating from his 1651 work, *Leviathan*. He argued that without a strong central authority to maintain order, human existence would be chaotic and violent, driven by selfishness and a fear of death. In Hobbes's view, people are inherently self-interested and prone to conflict, making life insecure and harsh. This contrasts sharply with other political philosophers such as John Locke, who saw humans as more rational and cooperative, capable of mutual respect and collective progress under social contracts.

Khozein shared that rooting in a more hopeful outlook for humanity helps him to engage with business partners and colleagues with greater optimism and mutual respect. However, he cautions that such hope must be rooted in both faith and evidence. With the right discernment, we can align with others who share our values and develop a guiding hope, one not centered in naivete but rather grounded in reality. Leaders can cultivate such hope and alignment by engaging in open, honest dialogue, involving their teams in decision-making, and acknowledging the evidence of progress—no matter how incremental.

Khozein spoke in depth about balancing both evidence-based logic and a more intuitive, relational approach. This intersection of science and spirituality is also a core concept in the Bahá'í Faith, offering a profound framework for investing and business, one that blends empirical rigor with deeper human values. Science can drive innovation, efficiency, and measurable outcomes, while spirituality inspires purpose, ethical intention, and a long-term vision anchored in meaning beyond mere profit. Together, they can empower leaders and investors to create enterprises that are not only financially sustainable but also regenerative and aligned with the well-being of people and the planet. This synergy invites a holistic approach where analytical insight and spiritual wisdom coalesce to guide decision-making with clarity, compassion, and hope for a better future—all while rooting into the present moment.

When it comes to practical advice for leading with hope grounded in reality, Khozein emphasized how mindfulness practices connect us to the sanctity of everyday life. As Khozein put it, "When every moment of your day feels like a spiritual experience, it energizes you and fosters growth—not just professionally but as a human being." It's this spirit that Khozein aims to bring to his workplace. He knows that not every single second of life will feel peaceful, holy, and profound, but he sees spirituality as something more inclusive and all-encompassing. He urges leaders to think about the work itself as a spiritual experience and of spirituality as fully integrated—not something reserved for moments of meditation or personal reflection but as something felt in the trenches of daily tasks.

Khozein's optimistic vision for an abundant workplace challenges us to rethink the way we interact within organizations. Leaders must move beyond transactional relationships and create environments where trust, reciprocity, and shared purpose take center stage. Where evidence-based reason blends with a relational, values-driven approach—and where hope for the future is rooted in mindfulness and presence.

As Khozein put it, "Believing in a fundamentally better way of being—both individually and collectively—is not just aspirational. It's essential for creating workplaces where employees and organizations can truly thrive."

Building a Community of Hope

For more insights into creating hopeful and inclusive cultures, let's look to Ben Powell, founder of Agora Partnerships, an accelerator dedicated to empowering social entrepreneurs across Latin America. Powell's mission is to transform good ideas into new models that address societal challenges more effectively than the status quo. His work is guided by a belief in the power of inclusive ecosystems, shared ownership, and human agency to drive meaningful change.

In our conversation, we explored how leaders can harness the power of hope to cultivate inclusive cultures and the benefits of doing so. Powell's responses offer a vision for how hope can transform workplaces and empower individuals.

- **Positivity in leadership:** Powell emphasized that positivity is one of the most powerful emotions in any organization. It instills a sense of agency—the belief that individuals can make a difference and contribute meaningfully. According to Powell, glimmers of positivity can always be found and modeled, and these can inspire and animate your organizational values and stated company mission and vision.

  He believes that healthy cultures are built on shared optimism and collective purpose, rejecting the more individualistic approaches that he considers toxic and unsustainable. Instead, great organizations can act as living organisms—dynamic, adaptable, and grounded in mutually beneficial values that inspire higher aspirations so that the sum can truly be greater than its parts.

  But to truly embed hope within an organization, leaders must do more than just talk about positivity in core values; they must live them. "Good organizations are constantly evolving, pivoting, and moving," Powell said. This dynamism challenges us to work and lead teams as an organic whole, inspiring individuals while remaining focused on their collective mission.

- **Rituals and relationships:** To foster community and shared purpose at Agora Partnerships, Powell and his leadership team organized retreats where participants engaged in meaningful rituals. One particularly moving tradition was a bonfire ceremony in which attendees placed a log on the fire and publicly shared their personal commitments—not business pitches or return-on-investment goals but their deeper purpose and the problems they felt dedicated to solving.

  These retreats embodied the spirit of a living organism. They created a space where people could connect as individuals, not just as entrepreneurs or colleagues. By celebrating relationships and fostering trust, these rituals galvanized hope and belonging, reminding participants of the deeper individual threads comprising their shared mission.

- **Unstructured time and iteration:** At first, Powell's team overstructured the agenda at these retreats. But through iteration, they found that allowing space for organic interactions strengthened relationships and sparked creativity. He highlighted the importance of getting more comfortable with iteration—an essential skill, especially for young institutions and start-ups. The ability to pivot and embrace change strengthens organizations while reinforcing the culture of hope and possibility.

- **From transactional to relational leadership:** Powell stressed the importance of shifting from a transactional to a relational approach in leadership and management. "When we focus on building trust and genuinely getting to know one another," Powell said, "we can achieve incredible things together."

  Powell's vision of hope in the workplace challenges leaders to reimagine how they foster inclusion, purpose, and trust. By creating cultures where individuals connect to a larger mission, leaders can catalyze inclusion and unlock extraordinary potential—not just for their organizations but for society as a whole.

  As Powell put it, "Hope is the galvanizing force that transforms relationships, strengthens organizations, and makes the seemingly impossible achievable."

Final Reflections on Hope

Hope is more than a lofty ideal; it's a lifesaving force. It keeps people from succumbing to despair, organizations from shutting their doors, and communities from fracturing under pressure. According to research by the positivity psychologist Dr. Charles Richard ("Rick") Snyder, hope consists of three components:

1. Setting a goal.
2. Identifying pathways to achieve it.
3. Fostering a sense of agency—the belief that "I can do this."[11]

Speaker and author Brené Brown has picked up Snyder's mantle of positive psychology, as she studies vulnerability, empathy, and courage. Brown's insights into hope are particularly illuminating. She emphasizes that hope is not an emotion but a cognitive-behavioral process.

"Right now, the thing that is helping the most is micro-dosing hope," Brown wrote in *The Gifts of Imperfection.* "I have no access to big hope right now. However, I am asking myself how I can support the people around me . . . Doing the smallest next right thing is hard, but sometimes it's all we've got."[12]

This idea of micro-dosing hope—finding small actionable steps forward—is profoundly relevant. In moments of crisis, hope works not in grand gestures but through small intentional acts that reorient us toward courage, kindness, and care. The kind of can-do approach to hope championed by both Snyder and Brown can truly transform individuals and companies both. That's because it's rooted in action and buoyed by possibility.

This perspective aligns with modern research from Princeton University, the Hope Research Center, and more.[13] Studies from these institutions show that hope can change patterns, counteracting the effects of trauma and promoting healing and resilience in both individuals and communities. In 2024, Princeton's Office of Religious Life hosted an event titled "The Healing Power of Hope" that offered insights into maintaining mental and emotional resilience during internal and external struggles.[14] The resounding message was clear: By fostering a sense of possibility, hope provides a buffer against despair and empowers us to take meaningful action.

Speaking of academic studies into the intersection of business and hope, from 2015 through 2017, I had the privilege of serving as a teaching assistant for Jennifer Aaker, an American behavioral scientist and professor at the Stanford Graduate School of Business, renowned for her research on time, money, and happiness. During this time, I gained invaluable insights into her groundbreaking research on concepts such as hope and awe.

In particular, Aaker emphasized how experiencing awe and beauty has the remarkable ability to expand our sense of time and enhance our well-being. Whether marveling at the vastness of the Grand Canyon or the breathtaking view from the Eiffel Tower, most of us have felt moments of profound wonder. In a series of experiments, Aaker worked with psychologists Melanie Rudd and Kathleen Vohs to find that awe-inspiring moments can slow our perception of time, making us feel like we have more of it.

This shift not only increases patience and life satisfaction but also reframes our motivations and decision-making. Namely, the researchers found that awe makes people more willing to help others, prefer experiences over material possessions, and stay present in the moment.[15] As Aaker explains, "When you feel awe, you are experiencing a positive emotion that feels vast and big, capable of altering your view of the world and how you use your time, ultimately leading to greater fulfillment."[16]

Ultimately, hope encourages us to think expansively while integrating our vision into our daily actions, both big and small. It also challenges us to remain realistic and grounded. We may never achieve a human utopia on earth, but hope doesn't require us to remake the world in some sparkly image of perfection. Instead, we can stay focused on making the next positive changes, both personally and professionally, that support those around us and our vision of integrated, healthy progress.

Futurist Kevin Kelly, cofounder of *Wired* magazine, calls this concept *protopia*. Rather than disempowering ourselves by either focusing solely on crises or dreaming of an impossible utopia, Kelly urges us to strive for a world where incremental progress leads to tangible, and sometimes even transformational, improvement. This vision encourages us to prototype the future we want to create, embracing experimentation and collaboration. By prioritizing small positive changes, we can build a foundation for sustained transformation.

A New Global Framework Is Taking Place

We live in an extraordinary time, a moment of both unprecedented crisis and ripe possibility. As existing systems break down, a clear vision simultaneously emerges—one that prioritizes collaboration, equity, and sustainability instead of competition, exploitation, and short-term gains.

Hope is the bridge that connects us to this new reality. It is the foundation on which we can build systems that honor our interconnectedness and shared humanity. My mother's unwavering belief in the power of hope is a legacy that I carry forward. It's a reminder that even in moments of uncertainty, we can choose to believe in the possibility of something better.

And so, when my friend asked me what my mother would make of this moment in human history, I knew what she would say. She would urge us all to hold on to hope—not as a passive wish but as an active, living force. She would remind us that hope is what transforms ideas into actions and dreams into realities. It is what allows us to see not just the world as it is but the world as it could be.

I began this chapter with a quote by the famous late primatologist Jane Goodall, who literally wrote *The Book of Hope.*[17] This work, subtitled *A Survival Guide for Trying Times*, explains why Goodall sustained her hope for the future of humanity, despite ominous scientific predictions about the climate and the Earth's natural systems on which we all depend.

Goodall's action-oriented optimism reminds us that real hope is not a spectator state of mind but rather a passionate mobilization to get up and join forces with the world around us. This kind of hope dares us to transcend fear and indifference by taking deliberate steps toward building a better future through our relationships and our work. I find her words a powerful reminder that optimism is not just a nice feeling; it's a courageous pledge to action, a belief in the possibility of change, and a summons to support solutions of hope—whether they're grand and sweeping or just a tiny next step in the direction we want to go. This kind of hope keeps us going and inspires those around us.

As we wrap up this first pillar of the HEAL framework, I leave you with some final takeaways for leaders who want to infuse more hope into their work:

- **Anchor your organization in shared values.** Clearly articulate and live your core values. Let them guide decisions, foster alignment, and inspire your team.
- **Cultivate community.** Create rituals and spaces that allow individuals to connect on a deeper level, celebrating their shared purpose and commitment.
- **Embrace dynamism and iteration.** Recognize that organizations, like living organisms, must evolve. Be open to change, and use it as an opportunity to strengthen your culture.
- **Prioritize relationships over transactions.** Invest in trust and relational leadership to galvanize hope, build stronger teams, and achieve collective success.

My personal *hope* is that this chapter has inspired you to reflect more deeply on what this principle means to you as a leader in your profession and in your personal life. In these uncertain times, there is a profound connection among hope, the challenges we face, and our ability to shape our individual and collective futures.

I encourage you to consider the meaningful conversations you can initiate within your organization, business, and society at large about cultivating hope and fostering a vision for a better tomorrow. Begin to act by reading the reality around you. Through collective reflection, we can create a shared visual—a rich picture of the challenges and opportunities in our communities, organizations, and world today. The next step could be to align yourself with like-minded people who can support you on this path to fostering hope at home and in the workplace.

Take a moment to reflect on these themes of hope, as a leader, a business owner, an investor, and a community member. Add another layer to your reflections by thinking about your goals and aspirations for the end of the month and the end of the year—and how these insights into hope can inform and inspire your journey toward those goals.

REFLECTION QUESTIONS

- What gives you hope in your personal and professional life, and why?
- Can you identify practical, meaningful steps to strengthen hope in your everyday life?
- How might you as a leader begin to foster this culture of hope in your organization today?
- Can you initiate small group discussions in your workplace teams, at home, and in your community to reflect collectively on hope? How can these discussions inform active collaborations with others toward building a better future?
- How can you assess the levels of hope and optimism within your team?
- How can you encourage more open, unstructured time for reflection, connection, or innovation?
- How do you ensure that all voices are heard and valued, especially those from underrepresented or marginalized groups?
- What feedback mechanisms can you introduce to measure how employees feel about their work, the culture, and their sense of purpose?

CHAPTER 5

Empathy: From Chaos to Coherence

Forces beyond your control can take away everything you possess except one thing, your freedom to choose how you will respond to the situation.

—VIKTOR E. FRANKL, *MAN'S SEARCH FOR MEANING*

After surviving the Auschwitz concentration and extermination camp complex, acclaimed Austrian psychologist Viktor Frankl went on to found a branch of psychotherapy based on meaning. It was his belief that atrocities such as the Holocaust thrive best when people feel overwhelmed by incoherence when they lack the shared meaning that comes through empathy, connection, and mutual understanding.

I take comfort in Frankl's words these days. The tumult of modern times may feel overwhelming, but it is within this very chaos that the seeds of renewal and integration are sown. To me, another writing attributed to 'Abdu'l-Bahá also captures the essence of our collective journey from chaos to coherence:

> Although outwardly, cataclysms are hard to understand and to endure, yet there lies a great wisdom behind them, which

> appears later. All the visible material events are interrelated with invisible spiritual forces. The infinite phenomena of creation are as interdependent as the links of a chain. When certain links become rusty, they are broken by unseen forces, to be replaced by newer and better ones.[1]

In this journey, empathy, the second part of the HEAL (hope, empathy, abundance, and legacy) framework, emerges as a powerful tool for navigating the turbulent waters of change. By cultivating our capacity to share, or at least recognize, the feelings of others, we create bridges of understanding amid the chaos. Empathy allows us to see beyond our individual perspectives, fostering a broader viewpoint and sense of interconnectedness, both crucial for moving toward greater coherence. It enables us to recognize the shared human experience within the apparent division and disorder, paving the way for collective healing, reconciliation, and transformation.

When I think of the pillar of empathy, I conjure the image of holding hands. This visual beautifully illustrates the process of integration. Just as individuals come together to support and uplift one another, so, too, must organizations and societies join forces to create a unified whole. Such collective effort requires shared goals, consistent communication, and a commitment to mutual support—and all of that is rooted in mutual empathy.

These days, such uplifting images of mutual support can seem to be in short supply. Global news reflects more than ever the rise of pressing issues: extreme (and growing) wealth disparity, poverty, war, climate change, political strife, gender and racial inequity—the list goes on. In response, many may feel a sense of helplessness and either give up altogether or seek ways to fix the current global crisis.

Although this growing "tide of conflict and disorder"[2] seems to intensify with each passing day, it also signals a cycle of breakdown and renewal that can play a key role in societal progress. With these dual forces at play, we are called to examine not only the external transformations unfolding around us but also the internal shifts required to align with a higher purpose and a more unified vision of humanity.

Those internal forces are much quieter than the distracting noise of external crises, and that is by design. It's never a surprise to me when the concept of empathy comes under attack by those most poised to benefit from inequality, exploitation, and extraction. Luckily, as leaders, founders, and investors, we are in a powerful position to shape organizations and collaborations. Although it is important to be aware of the many external changes, it's crucial for us to remain connected to that inner guidance and to one another. Here is where empathy comes in.

Forces of Disintegration and Integration

Today we are witnessing two powerful and opposing forces shaping our world: disintegration and integration. On the one hand, *disintegration* manifests in widening divides—economic, social, and cultural—that strain the fabric of communities and nations. On the other hand, *integration* calls for creative solutions and collaborative efforts to rebuild connections and foster shared progress. Before we explore what integration might look like and the potential pathways forward, it's important to first examine the evidence of disintegration.

Recent US and global data reflect socioeconomic patterns of wealth inequality, income disparity, and complex societal challenges. For example, according to Federal Reserve data, as of the first quarter of 2025, the top 1 percent of households in the United States held 31.6 percent of the country's wealth.[3] A 2024 report noted that billionaire wealth has grown significantly, and continues to grow, with the global charitable organization Oxfam predicting the emergence of at least five trillionaires within the next decade.[4]

As corruption and political polarization intensify, economic insecurities and protests also rise. The data just cited reveal how the unraveling of civilization today is deeply rooted in the pervasive condition of materialism. The materialistic view of reality has in many ways shaped human consciousness and societal structures. Yet this perspective has reached its limits—society and our leaders have been unable to resolve the mounting crises of inequity, environmental degradation, and spiritual emptiness.

In this disintegration, however, lies an opportunity for integration—a chance to reimagine and rebuild a world civilization grounded in spiritual principles, empathy, and collective unity. The Guardian of the Bahá'í Faith described this era as the "coming of age of the entire human race,"[5] marking a pivotal moment in the evolution of humanity. Just as an individual progresses from childhood to adulthood—gaining greater understanding, responsibility, and the ability to cooperate with others—humanity is undergoing a similar transformation. This means that rather than remaining divided by outdated systems of conflict, prejudice, and competition, we have an opportunity to develop a more mature, unified, and cooperative global society.

The Bahá'í Revelation offers a framework for this transformation, emphasizing an "organic and spiritual unity that transcends material concerns." In other words, true unity is not just about political alliances, economic cooperation, or technological advancements—it goes much deeper than that. It's about recognizing that all human beings are fundamentally connected, not just through shared resources and economies but also at the spiritual level. This perspective can encourage people to move beyond short-term material, self-centered interests, such as wealth, power, or national identity, and instead focus on the well-being of the entire human family, based on a sense of deep empathy and interconnectivity.

In this vision of unity, diversity is not erased but celebrated, and differences—whether cultural, racial, or religious—become sources of strength rather than division. The goal is not simply coexistence but an active and dynamic process of building a world where justice, equity, empathy, and cooperation become the foundation of human interactions.[6]

Around the world, there is evidence of a growing consciousness centered on sustainability, equity, empathy, and interconnectedness. As a business leader, I see this across individuals, organizations, and investment strategies. For example, companies such as Patagonia exemplify this shift by embedding ethical and sustainable practices into their business models. Through initiatives like its Fair Trade Certified program, Patagonia ensures that workers in its supply chain receive fair wages and safe working conditions, reinforcing its commitment to social equity and environmental responsibility.[7]

In my conversation with Julian MacQueen of Innisfree Hotels, he shared a core principle that has shaped his company's culture: checking paranoid fantasies. He defined *paranoid fantasies* as unverified feelings or assumptions often stemming from interpersonal interactions that can easily spiral into unnecessary anxiety or conflict. For instance, if a colleague unexpectedly walks past without greeting you, your mind might immediately assume the worst—perhaps they're upset with you, or maybe something you did has damaged the relationship. However, as MacQueen pointed out, these thoughts are often baseless fabrications of the mind that, if left unchecked, can damage relationships and workplace dynamics. To address this, Innisfree executives and team leaders encourage employees to directly ask if a perceived slight or misunderstanding is real. Normalizing and reinforcing this kind of open communication fosters a culture of transparency, connection, and emotional resilience.

By mindfully integrating the practice of checking paranoid fantasies, Innisfree Hotels exemplifies how fostering trust and psychological safety within an organization directly contributes to a more compassionate, values-driven workplace. This shift underscores a broader movement toward evaluating businesses not only by their bottom line but also by their commitment to human-centered leadership and ethical impact—one that recognizes that kindness, integrity, and emotional well-being are not just ideals but essential components of sustainable success.

Increasingly, organizations are being evaluated not only on financial performance but also on the depth of their compassion, culture, and overall commitment to employee well-being. To attract and retain top talent, companies increasingly recognize that a healthy, communicative, empathetic, and emotionally intelligent workplace is not just beneficial for individuals but also a key driver of long-term success. MacQueen's method of addressing paranoid fantasies is rooted in spiritual values—compassion, trust, empathy, and honest dialogue—all of which contribute to creating workplaces where employees are valued and supported. By integrating these principles, companies mitigate misunderstandings while cultivating environments where people thrive, and in turn the companies flourish. This is also taking place at scale through initiatives such as the United Nations Global Compact, the world's largest corporate sustainability initiative, mobilizing over twenty thousand corporate participants and stakeholders across 167 countries to adopt and implement socially responsible policies.[8]

Together, these examples reflect a global commitment to integrating sustainable and equitable practices into the fabric of business and investment. They signal a collective readiness for a more unified, ethical, and spiritually conscious reality—one where business success is increasingly defined by its positive impact on people and the planet.

How, might you ask? Let's find out next.

Coherence: A Pathway to Integration

Living amid the dual forces of disintegration and integration can become confusing and overwhelming. Chaotic forces of division abound during these times, but so much of that division depends on us closing our hearts through fear, greed, competition, and conflict. With empathy, a greater coherence is possible, which, in addition to hope, offers another key dimension for transformation, both at an individual and at an organizational level. Coherence refers to the formation of a unified whole.

The Bahá'í Universal House of Justice offers the following perspective:

> That a global civilization which is both materially and spiritually prosperous represents the next stage of a millennia-long process of social evolution provides a conception of history that endows every instance of social action with a particular purpose: to foster true prosperity, with its spiritual and material dimensions, among the diverse inhabitants of the planet. A concept of vital relevance, then,

> is the imperative to achieve a dynamic coherence between the practical and spiritual requirements of life.[9]

This quote highlights the necessity of integrating ethical, just, and sustainable principles into the systems governing economic and social life. Businesses and investments, traditionally viewed as purely material pursuits, increasingly serve as vehicles for manifesting spiritual values such as equity, justice, and compassion. In this light, social equity and sustainability are not just ethical business considerations; they can be profound expressions of a deeper spiritual consciousness materializing in the corporate world.

Companies such as Ben & Jerry's exemplify how corporate success can align with values of fairness, environmental stewardship, and social justice. Ben & Jerry's has long championed social justice causes, from supporting fair trade sourcing to advocating for racial and economic equity. By embedding these principles into its business model, the company has strengthened its brand reputation while also actively contributing to creating a more just society.[10]

Ben & Jerry's illustrates how integrating social equity into operations can go beyond idealistic aspiration to become a tangible, impactful strategy that benefits both society and business. All the organizations I connected with for this book (among many others) have created similar coherence by integrating a culture of empathy and shared meaning not only into their company values but also into their core strategy.

To guide such efforts, tools such as the Social Equity Impact Assessment[11] and the B Impact Assessment can provide frameworks for measuring and improving a company's social and environmental performance, ensuring accountability and continuous progress. These efforts signal a profound evolution in the corporate world, where material success and spiritual values such as justice, empathy, and equity are no longer seen as opposing forces but as mutually reinforcing elements of a prosperous civilization. By prioritizing the well-being of marginalized communities, ensuring fair treatment for all individuals, and aligning business goals with broader social values, companies contribute to a more just and sustainable global economy.

Beyond benefiting communities, this approach enhances long-term business resilience, reputation, and profitability. The growing alignment between ethical business practices and economic success illustrates the unfolding reality of a civilization striving toward both material and spiritual prosperity—one where equity, justice, empathy, and sustainability are not just ideals but fundamental pillars of progress.

Integrating Spiritual and Material Prosperity into Business and Investing

According to the Universal House of Justice, "To seek coherence between the spiritual and the material does not imply that the material goals of development are to be trivialized."[12] Rather, it calls for a more holistic approach, where financial success is not pursued in isolation from ethical and social considerations. In the world of business and investing, this translates into a shift from purely profit-driven strategies focused on shareholder primacy to models that balance profitability with sustainability and equity.

For example, socially responsible investing and corporate sustainability practice frameworks have gained traction as investors recognize that long-term financial health depends on ethical labor practices, environmental sustainability, and fair governance. Often such conscious investing strategies can change an entire company, or even an industry, for the better. For example, Calvert, a socially responsible investment firm, once played a pivotal role in influencing Dell's sustainability policies. In the early 2000s, Calvert filed a shareholder resolution requesting that Dell study the end-of-life impact of its computers. This action caught the attention of the CEO, Michael Dell himself, who invited Calvert representatives to discuss the issue. As a result of this engagement, Dell implemented a comprehensive recycling program that became the industry standard. This example demonstrates the power of socially responsible investing to prompt a major technology company to adopt more environmentally responsible practices and set an industry standard that drove broader corporate change.

Investors and corporate leaders cannot assume that Western capitalist frameworks are universally applicable or beneficial. The one-size-fits-all approach, where multinational corporations impose their structures on diverse economies, often leads to economic dependencies rather than genuine development. Consider the devastating impact of extractive industries such as the fossil fuel industry and mining companies on developing countries, where corporations have historically decimated natural resources without reinvesting in local economies. This model has often led to environmental degradation, social displacement, and economic disenfranchisement.

In contrast, impact investment funds such as Acumen[13] and Root Capital[14] take a different approach, focusing on empowering local entrepreneurs with capital and training tailored to their unique economic and cultural contexts. By rejecting a uniform model and instead fostering local agency, such investments create long-term, self-sustaining prosperity rather than purely short-term gains for external investors alone.

According to the Universal House of Justice, "When the material and spiritual dimensions of the life of a community are kept in mind and due attention is given to both scientific and spiritual knowledge, the tendency to reduce development to the mere consumption of goods and services and the naive use of technological packages is avoided."[15] This quote speaks directly to the current challenges of consumerism-driven economies, where success is often measured purely by GDP growth and corporate revenue rather than on well-being or environmental impact. In business, this insight challenges companies to move beyond traditional consumption-based models.

During my time at the Stanford Graduate School of Business, I organized a trip to Bhutan to explore the business of happiness through the lens of the country's focus on what they call Gross National Happiness. Bhutan created a practical way to measure their national progress based on this idea of collective well-being rather than on material gains. During that trip to Bhutan, we got to see firsthand how a governing philosophy aimed at happiness can help foster both community cohesion and workplace loyalty through shared values and community engagement rather than solely through financial incentives.

Bhutan's story offers a living case study at the intersection of spirituality, investing, and business—a nation seeking to integrate practical policy and economic progress with deeper notions of happiness. The concept of spiritual consultants, introduced during my visit, raises this question: *What if all companies adopted practices rooted in spiritual values?*

Bhutan's Gross National Happiness framework invites organizations to embed sustainability, cultural preservation, and environmental ethics into their operations, challenging the relentless pursuit of growth for growth's sake. This intentional approach to development highlights intriguing possibilities for businesses worldwide, suggesting that a spiritual underpinning can offer not just ethical grounding but also resilience and a broader sense of impact within society.

Yet Bhutan's journey is one of contradictions as much as inspiration. The country negotiates the ongoing tension between tradition and modernity, with individuals and organizations alike navigating the challenge of sustaining cultural identity while embracing necessary progress. Although Gross National Happiness influences business decisions, some locals question whether its principles are always authentically realized or whether they sometimes amount to happiness-washing. Nevertheless, the national focus on well-being reverberates beyond metrics, fostering spaces for vulnerability and authenticity—even as society grapples with issues such as mental health that are often hidden beneath national narratives. Bhutan's pursuit reminds us that bringing spirituality into the realms of investment and business is an ongoing, imperfect, and deeply human practice—one that may hold keys to reconciling impact, profit, and purpose in other communities as well.

Redefining Prosperity in Business and Investing

The path forward in business and investing is not about choosing between financial success and ethical responsibility—it's about integrating them. When economic models are designed with both scientific understanding and ethical insight, they create prosperity that is materially, socially, and spiritually enriching.

From responsible artificial intelligence development to circular economies and shareholder activism, businesses and investors today have unprecedented opportunities to redefine prosperity. By rejecting the passive acceptance of consumerism and short-term profit-seeking, we find opportunities to actively build an economic system that aligns with deeper values of justice, sustainability, and human well-being.

This is not some utopian ideal; it's already happening. The businesses and investors leading this charge are not only proving that ethical decision-making is viable but also demonstrating that it's essential for long-term resilience in an ever-changing world.

In the intersection of individual and organizational transformation, coherence and empathy play crucial roles, mainly in terms of aligning personal development and organizational change processes. Whether or not you hold a formal leadership title, fostering coherence and empathy within an organization requires intentional strategies. Practices that contribute to a more unified and purpose-driven workplace include aligning goals with values, rallying around a shared *why*, maintaining consistent communication, cultivating cultural coherence, and establishing empathetic feedback loops. These principles apply not only to those in leadership positions but also to anyone looking to create a positive and cohesive work environment.

In particular, the alignment of goals with values is critical because it fosters a shared sense of purpose, ensuring that personal and organizational growth contribute to collective progress. Without this coherence, businesses risk becoming reactive rather than intentional. Companies that successfully integrate values into their operations build stronger organizational cultures while also creating significant competitive advantages.

Connecting to the *Why* Beneath Our Actions

One way to deepen this alignment is by connecting to the *why* beneath our actions.

As an investor, Stephen DeBerry, managing director of Bronze, aligns his own business decisions to the values and goals—the *why*—that matter to him. He has seen over the years how such alignment allows companies to create products and services that genuinely serve humanity. That is the kind of venture Bronze wants to support.

In particular, the firm focuses on addressing disparities in wealth and well-being by investing in businesses and real estate that close opportunity gaps, particularly in marginalized communities. DeBerry, a venture capitalist and an impact investor, advocates for a model where financial returns are not just measured in terms of wealth accumulation but also in social progress. His work challenges traditional investment paradigms, demonstrating that capital can be a tool for equity and justice when deployed with intentionality. DeBerry also actively advocates for the idea that love is a competitive advantage, and he integrates this concept into his investment decision-making process. DeBerry has a life philosophy and mantra of "joy and ease" that has been incredibly inspiring to me.

During my work with One Planet Group investing in early-stage companies and acquiring businesses, we would ask the companies that we invested in to sign a betterment-of-the-world agreement with the intention of creating alignment among us as investors, the companies, and the broader community.

By understanding the true purpose behind an entrepreneur's or organization's work, we can foster a culture of compassion and strategic support, one where shared purpose becomes a key factor in decision-making. Salesforce exemplifies this corporate dynamic through its 1-1-1 philanthropic framework. The customer relationship technology company dedicates 1 percent of its equity, product, and employee time, respectively, to social impact initiatives.[16] This approach benefits communities while strengthening the company's culture and brand loyalty.

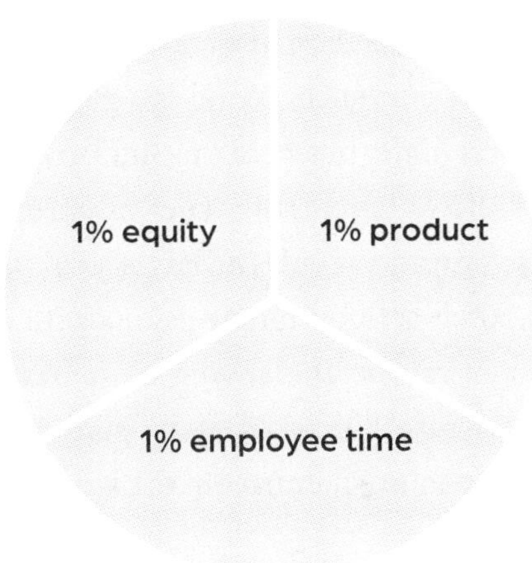

Applying Values Alignment Beyond Entrepreneurship

Although this concept is often discussed in entrepreneurial settings, it's just as relevant for leaders, employees, investors, policymakers, and institutional decision-makers. Whether you're running a start-up, leading a Fortune 500 company, managing an investment portfolio, or working in a nonprofit, ensuring that your organization's goals align with a broader mission enhances resilience, engagement, and long-term success.

Ultimately, businesses and institutions that operate with a clear, purpose-driven framework do more than just survive market fluctuations—they thrive by building trust, fostering innovation, and creating lasting impact. Aligning values with strategy is not just an ethical choice; it's a blueprint for sustainable and meaningful success in an evolving global economy.

Author Simon Sinek, in his influential work on leadership and purpose mentioned earlier, emphasizes that companies driven by a strong *why* inspire greater loyalty, engagement, and long-term success. In a company's mission, the *why* represents the core purpose or reason for its existence, acting as a guiding principle that connects all aspects of the business. As Sinek explains, organizations that start with *why* create coherence by ensuring that everyone in the company understands the larger goal they're working toward, aligning their actions and decisions with the company's overall mission and values. This shared sense of purpose fosters unity among employees while also strengthening the organization's ability to make a meaningful impact in the world.

Empathy and Purpose

Empathy and purpose, when woven together in the realms of spirituality, investing, and business, create a powerful foundation for meaningful leadership and ethical action. By fully understanding and sharing in the experiences of others—be they customers, colleagues, or communities—leaders can align business strategies with a higher sense of purpose, ensuring that decisions not only drive profit but also foster genuine connection and positive impact.

Organizations that embed empathy into their core operational values are better equipped to build trust, nurture loyalty, and innovate solutions that address real human needs. Purpose-driven entrepreneurs, guided by empathic insight, consistently prioritize integrity and service, bridging financial success and spiritual fulfillment to create ventures that uplift everyone involved.

One notable pioneer cultivating a deeper purpose within organizations is Ranjay Gulati, professor of business administration at Harvard Business School and author of *Deep Purpose: The Heart and Soul of High-Performance Companies. Deep Purpose* makes the case that a revolutionary approach to business does exist, one that delivers game-changing results for both companies and society alike: the serious and deep pursuit of purpose.

In his practical book, Gulati argues that companies must embed purpose much more deeply than they currently do, treating it as a radically new operating system for the enterprise. When companies practice deep purpose, furthering their organizations' reasons for being, it can revolutionize how they do business and deliver impressive performance benefits that reward customers, suppliers, employees, shareholders, and communities.[17]

According to Gulati, a stronger commitment to purpose is vital not only for the success of individual companies but also for the future of humanity. At a time when capitalism faces intense scrutiny and trust in business remains low, purpose can act as a transformative framework—one that boosts performance while creating meaningful value for society. This visionary approach is precisely what businesses, and the world at large, need now more than ever.

Although many leaders prioritize the future, the most successful organizations are also deeply rooted in their history, values, and purpose. Conducting an audit of a company's founding principles and original mission can help leaders decide what to preserve and what to leave behind, ensuring that progress is anchored in authenticity and clarity of purpose. Creating intentional space to reflect on mission alignment is crucial for any organization seeking authentic impact. Such pauses allow leaders and teams to assess whether day-to-day efforts and programs genuinely advance the stated purpose, surfacing gaps and opportunities for realignment. Regularly engaging in this reflective practice ensures that resources, culture, and strategic priorities remain connected to the organization's core mission, fostering clarity, motivation, and sustained progress.

Balancing Purpose and Profit

Purpose-driven companies aim to address societal and environmental problems while generating wealth, creating win-win scenarios. However, this journey is often fraught with challenges, as businesses struggle to balance purpose with profitability.

The goal is to empower employees while maintaining operational discipline. Resolving this tension is key to fostering innovation while ensuring direction and accountability. Recently, we have seen more management experiments, such as self-managed teams and matrix structures, as leaders seek tailored approaches that provide structure without suppressing creativity.[18]

Start-ups possess a unique, intangible energy—a soul—that fosters passion, collaboration, and innovation. This sense of shared purpose inspires employees, early customers, and investors, driving engagement and growth. However, as organizations scale, this spirit often fades, leaving a noticeable void. Sustaining this culture is crucial for long-term success. Start-ups also frequently struggle to scale, even when they have promising resources, customers, and cash flow. Successful scaling requires navigating complex challenges, including operational structure, leadership alignment, and cultural preservation, to avoid derailment.

Deep Impact Economy

Charly Kleissner, an investor, an entrepreneur, and a pioneer in the impact investing space, offers profound insights into the intersection of spirituality, investing, and business. He identifies fundamental design flaws in the current economic and financial systems that obstruct the realization of universal love and oneness. Kleissner explains that the core flaw in the economic system is the misguided belief in exponential growth on a planet with finite resources, which inherently disregards the interconnectedness of all sentient beings and nature. Similarly, he says that the financial system's deadly design flaw is its singular focus on maximizing financial returns, often at the expense of everything else, thereby neglecting the broader well-being that stems from a sense of oneness. These systems, according to Kleissner, are driven by an anthropocentric, very human-centric consciousness that prevents humanity from addressing critical global challenges effectively.

To rectify these deeply ingrained issues, Kleissner advocates for the deep impact economy. He defines this as an approach that is "systemic in nature, treating not just the symptoms but also the hard design flaws of these other systems; it's with the level of consciousness that actually takes into account who we really are and our responsibility of being human." This deep impact economy envisions impact investors, impact entrepreneurs, and impact intermediaries working together within supportive regulatory frameworks to foster businesses that create systemic positive change.

Kleissner emphasizes that a crucial part of the investment decision-making process is detaching from the outcome, because "it is difficult to predict with your intellect only what is going to happen." Instead, he urges individuals to "listen to what channels are opening up for you to tap into this global consciousness."

These channels refer to the emergent, intuitive insights and possibilities that arise when one lets go of predetermined results and is open to sensing the future. This approach contrasts with conventional, linear extrapolation, instead serving as a soft power mechanism to build shared visions, embracing qualities such as humility, tenacity, empathy, compassion, and discipline from leaders.

By embracing this global consciousness and understanding universal oneness, individuals can transcend a purely human-centric perspective, leading to greater empathy toward all people. Kleissner personally found that cultivating compassion requires "hard work," highlighting its essential role. He views mindfulness not merely as a self-serving practice, but "necessary to be of service to other people and to change systems," asserting that ego-based practices are misaligned with universal energies. For Kleissner, the impact of someone's life is a direct expression of who they really are, not who they think or feel they are; and the trajectory of humanity is a direct expression of humanity's consciousness. Therefore, he has been dedicating his life towards helping elevate humanity's consciousness. For Kleissner, the best way to do this is for people to work on themselves, on their inner landscape, which leads to the clarity, inner peace and joy, necessary to show up for the outer work, as inner and outer transformation become one—a cosmic dance grounded in equanimity, humility, and compassion. On the business side, this expanded awareness allows leaders to consider a "holistic picture" of everyone a company touches, from suppliers and clients to customers and investors, striving to enrich the entire value chain.

This expanded awareness allows leaders to consider a holistic picture of everyone a company touches, from suppliers and clients to customers and investors, striving to enrich the entire value chain. I've had the opportunity to collaborate with Kleissner around the great work he has engaged in building a community of other investors who care about the deep impact economy through groups such as the 100 percent impact group within Toniic. Other networks, such as Synergos's Spiritual Civilization Collaborative Community,[19] also engage philanthropists and investors around bringing inner work to outer action. Among the programs that nurture this spirit of reflection is the chaplaincy program within Echoing Green, where I am a fellow—a place that tends the inner life of social entrepreneurs, inviting them to root their work in the depth of their own values and to find harmony between purpose and practice.

The current era calls for leaders who can catalyze collective, cocreative leadership, building networks of trust and sensing emergent futures. Kleissner's hope for a better future is rooted in humanity's collective agency to embrace this elevated consciousness and drive systemic change.

The Power of Belonging

A clear shared purpose grounded in empathy can generate a profound sense of belonging and fulfillment in a team, an organization, or a cooperative partnership. As leaders, founders, and investors, we can nurture this shared purpose and belonging by cultivating a sense of psychological safety, especially when it comes to expressing ideas and concerns. For true belonging to flourish, everyone must be genuinely heard—their voices actively listened to, understood, and reflected in the shared mission.

Imagine leading a values-driven venture capital firm where commitment extends beyond financial success to the holistic well-being of portfolio companies and their founders. Here partners and senior investors mentor entrepreneurs with empathy, guiding them through challenges while supporting their mental and emotional balance amid the pressures of scaling a business. During critical times such as fundraising or product launches, the team steps in collaboratively to relieve stress, offer strategic support, and foster an environment where founders can recharge without fear of stalled momentum.

This ecosystem of trust requires active listening, careful attention to your own and others' values and goals, an open exchange of ideas, and a mutual affirmation of the organization's shared *why*. Leaders can model integrity and reliability through clear communication and consistent, values-aligned actions. When investors take this approach, their firms enjoy sustained growth while deeply supporting entrepreneurs and attracting other founders who seek partnerships beyond capital—collaborations rooted in trust, shared purpose, and inclusive belonging.

Such integration of purpose requires honoring the deeper principles that sustain empathy in business—ways of being that encourage proactive care, maintain balance, and cultivate a virtues-based framework to navigate challenges without ethical compromise. This approach nurtures lasting belonging and collaboration, where everyone's voice is essential and every perspective is respected.

Consistent Communication and Organizational Coherence

Clear and consistent communication is critical for maintaining organizational coherence. Beyond simply sharing information, this requires a foundation of empathy—truly understanding and valuing the perspectives and experiences of team members. Effective leaders actively listen, creating space for everyone to have a voice and ensuring that these voices are both heard and meaningfully integrated into decision-making processes. When a team member's input aligns with the organization's shared *why*—its vision, purpose, and mission—it's not only acknowledged but also acted upon, demonstrating respect and reinforcing trust.

This approach fosters deeper connection, belonging, and engagement because individuals are seen and valued. It transforms communication from a one-way transmission into a dynamic dialogue that strengthens alignment and shared ownership. Effective leaders serve as great teachers and compassionate communicators. They model clarity and empathy while holding themselves and others accountable to the organization's core values, reinforcing a culture where purposeful collaboration thrives.

Workplace culture plays a crucial role in shaping employee engagement, work relationships, and overall job satisfaction. It's the foundation that determines an organization's short- and long-term success. Culture impacts the quality of products and services while deeply affecting the well-being of those within the organization—whether for good or for ill.

Sometimes a leader inherits a culture lacking in empathy, purpose, and coherence. The good news is that culture is not static; it's something that we, as leaders, have the power to shape and improve. In today's corporate landscape, stress, burnout, and disengagement have become pervasive workplace issues. Many companies attempt to address these challenges with flexible work policies, unlimited time off, and remote work options. However, these strategies alone are insufficient if workers do not feel connected to or represented by their company culture. Instead, organizations must focus on fostering a culture of belonging.

When employees enjoy their workplace, it benefits not only their mental health and well-being but also the organization—both financially and in other meaningful ways. By intentionally fostering a respectful, inspiring workplace culture, organizations create happier, more engaged, and more productive employees.

As a leader, you can contribute to a thriving workplace culture by addressing and reflecting on these essential questions:

- How does my organization's culture influence employees' satisfaction with their work environment?
- What steps can we take to improve it?
- How do I currently communicate with team members? What are some ways I could include more and better quality communications?
- How do we gather employee feedback, and what is our policy for evaluating and implementing that feedback?
- How does empathy for our employees and other stakeholders help build coherence (and/or the values of learning, innovation, and adaptability)?

Strong organizational cultures build coherence and consistency by firmly rooting their stated values in solid moral principles. This coherence emerges when leadership decisions, workplace dynamics, and company goals align with that shared ethical foundation.

An example of a leader who effectively built cultural cohesion at her company is Shabnam Mogharabi, cofounder and CEO of SoulPancake from 2009 to 2016. Along with her cofounder, actor Rainn Wilson, Mogharabi built SoulPancake into an award-winning media and entertainment brand with the mission of creating uplifting, inspiring video content that explores the depth of human experience across digital, social, television, and commercial platforms. In 2016, SoulPancake was acquired by Participant Media.

In an interview for this book, Mogharabi shared that she prioritized creating a strong workplace culture that cultivated a sense of belonging, engagement, and joy among employees. One of the core strategies she implemented was holding quarterly company-wide meetings to ensure transparency and alignment on business goals and direction. These gatherings provided employees with a clear understanding of where the company was headed and how they each contributed to its mission.

But they didn't just inform their employees of the company culture; they actively and empathetically involved these team members in the formation of that culture. To gain deeper insights into employee sentiment, SoulPancake conducted anonymous staff surveys, inviting team members to share their experiences and values, levels of joy at work, and areas that they feel needed improvement. This commitment to honest feedback helped shape a workplace that valued employee well-being and fosters a sense of personal belonging and both continuous and *coherent* collective improvement.

Mogharabi also integrated team-building activities and retreats into the company's culture. Twice a year, SoulPancake held retreats—including a one-day event focused on team cohesion and a more intensive three-day retreat. The longer retreats covered three key areas: company strategy for the upcoming year, an in-depth exploration of industry trends with expert insights, and strategies for strengthening workplace culture. By dedicating time to discuss and refine company values, SoulPancake reinforced its commitment to fostering a positive and collaborative work environment. In this way, SoulPancake demonstrated actionable empathy—getting genuinely curious about people's perspectives, experiences, and criticisms and actually integrating that feedback into company decision-making.

A significant component of the company's culture was its commitment to social impact. Under Mogharabi's leadership, employees participated in an annual volunteer day, engaging in activities to support local shelters and nonprofit organizations. In addition, the company encouraged regular donations of time and resources to community initiatives. This emphasis on giving back helped reinforce a collective sense of purpose and connection among employees as well as empathy for community stakeholders and neighbors.

Mogharabi firmly believes that the most significant factor that leaders can influence within an organization is its culture. Investing in a company's values, defining its purpose, and embedding those principles of empathy at every level of the organization ultimately strengthen the bond between employees and their workplace. By creating an environment where individuals belong, businesses can inspire loyalty, improve morale, and reinforce a deeper commitment to shared goals.

This approach was evident in SoulPancake's remarkably low employee turnover rate. When the company was acquired in 2016, it reported an annual turnover rate of fewer than 7 percent—a testament to the strong sense of belonging and purpose that kept employees engaged. Mogharabi attributes this success to the company's ability to cultivate a community-like atmosphere, where employees are valued and connected to a larger mission.

When actor and SoulPancake cofounder Rainn Wilson spoke to me for this book, he highlighted the importance of building something positive rather than just protesting negative or divisive trends and issues. He pointed out that being part of something bigger than oneself cultivates a sense of possibility and hope. For Wilson, the sacred can be found in the daily, including at work.

"When you are able to connect a business with its purpose, then a business is like a person," Wilson said. "When [as people] we're connected with our purpose, our thoughts are clearer, our actions are clearer, our spirit is lighter. We move forward every day; we're less likely to be overwhelmed and stuck."

Similarly, workplaces thrive when employees feel connected to and represented by their colleagues and the company's mission. A strong sense of community reduces stress, increases job satisfaction, and enhances overall productivity. At SoulPancake, this philosophy of empathy and coherence aligned corporate values and overall purpose. It remained at the heart of every decision, ensuring that employees saw their workplace not just as a job but also as a meaningful community where they each were seen, valued, and inspired.

Feedback Loops

Feedback loops are another vital component of coherence and empathy. By integrating individual insights into organizational strategies—and vice versa—we create a dynamic system of mutual learning and growth. This continuous exchange strengthens alignment and fosters shared purpose. It's also rooted in empathy and the coherence that comes when we remember how interconnected we are, and we make choices that result in mutually beneficial outcomes for all involved.

Examples of feedback loop practices to foster workplace coherence include the following:

- **360-degree feedback:** Collect feedback from peers, superiors, and subordinates to gain a comprehensive view of an employee's performance, based on both material results and corporate values.
- **Project postmortems:** Analyze completed projects to identify successes and areas for improvement, evaluating project alignment with company goals and values, and sharing insights with the team.

- **Employee engagement surveys:** Periodic surveys to gather feedback on workplace culture, satisfaction, and areas for improvement.
- **Continuous learning initiatives:** Encourage employees to share their knowledge, expertise, and personal values through internal training sessions and mentorship programs.

Practices such as 360-degree feedback, project postmortems, employee engagement surveys, and continuous learning initiatives are all valuable standard mechanisms for gathering insights and fostering workplace improvement, but it's not enough to simply collect feedback. Companies interested in a more enlightened bottom line also must consider how this feedback is delivered and received. Incorporating a spiritual perspective transforms these practices from mere evaluative tools into opportunities for deeper connection, growth, and alignment with shared values. By approaching feedback with empathy, self-awareness, and a focus on shared purpose, organizations can create a culture of trust and coherence. This approach ensures that feedback drives performance while *also* nurturing personal and collective well-being.

Julian MacQueen of Innisfree Hotels provides a compelling example of how integrating feedback tools and continuous learning initiatives can transform an organization into an industry leader. By training employees, from executives to housekeepers, Innisfree creates a culture where communication is transparent, respectful, and free of unnecessary conflict. This in turn allows employees to bring their whole, authentic selves to work, unburdened by learned behaviors from childhood that may no longer serve them in a professional setting. What sets Innisfree Hotels apart is how company leaders embed principles at every stage of the employee experience—from the hiring process to performance reviews to ongoing training. Prospective employees are introduced to the cooperative mode early on, ensuring that only those who align with the company's values become part of the organization. MacQueen emphasizes that fostering empathy, emotional intelligence, and critical self-awareness creates a self-sustaining workplace culture, one where employees naturally support one another and uphold the company's values. This approach has led to lower turnover, greater innovation, and stronger employee loyalty—all of which contribute to Innisfree's reputation as the hotel of choice for both employees and guests. Innisfree Hotels built this scalable, sustainable model through empathetic leadership. Their dedicated director of culture oversees training and development, alongside a growing team focused on embedding these practices enterprise-wide. They do this through effective, empathetic feedback loops that cultivate a culture of open communication, continuous improvement, and shared purpose, leading to greater coherence and alignment across teams and departments. By prioritizing employee well-being and emotional health, the company demonstrates that a culture of care is not just ethical leadership; it's also a strategy for long-term business success.

Another practical way that organizations can cultivate coherence and empathy is through a check-in process. This approach is about creating a space in each meeting for people to share how they're doing and whatever personal challenges or contexts they wish to disclose. For example, a person might share that they have a sick child at home. This informs other colleagues about potential scheduling challenges and helps teams to better support one another throughout the day. It also helps colleagues make more accurate assumptions about why, for example, a team member may seem more distracted or tense than usual (without guessing, projecting, or taking things personally). Without a check-in, people often fill in the gaps of understanding by making up a story to explain why someone, for example, looks tired, worried, or upset. The check-in enables coherence and empathy because it tests these assumptions and instead genuinely acknowledges where each person is, inside and outside of work.

Leadership and Management Practices

To cultivate empathetic coherence in a company, you need effective leadership. Inspiring leaders foster participation, recognize individual contributions, and actively seek out the resources needed to support their teams. All of this requires strong, internalized empathy, balanced with and aligned to the broader company mission. By creating an environment where everyone is valued and empowered, leaders can spark both personal and organizational transformation, even in resource-constrained settings. True leadership is not just about having the right tools—it's about rallying the team to innovate, adapt, and collectively build the foundation for lasting success.

I had the privilege of interviewing Bruno Monfils, a highly sought-after strategic adviser and mentor who works with Loyal VC, a Toronto-based firm that supports founders of investment companies, venture capitalists, and entrepreneurs in growing, diversifying, and redistributing wealth. Monfils is deeply passionate about mentoring leaders and developing strategies that focus on redistributing wealth in ways that serve humanity. Our conversation centered around the profound forces of integration and disintegration shaping the world today; how these forces intersect with individual and organizational work; and how he identifies opportunities to integrate more empathy, meaning, and coherence through his professional endeavors.

Monfils often reflects on whether business is conducted in a just and principled way. He noted that being people-centric and cultivating a mentality of truth-seeking are both essential to fostering this integration. Drawing from his twelve years at Amazon, he described how his Amazon team fostered an environment where decisions were based on facts and data, free from the influence of ego and politics.

This culture of open discussion, combined with the willingness to change when confronted with new evidence, exemplifies consultation from a spiritual perspective. Consultation is a decision-making tool that explores the perspectives of many rather than relying on a single voice. In consultation, participants come together not simply to defend their own positions but to foster fellowship, mutuality, and unity. Each person expresses their views freely and sincerely while recognizing that differing perspectives enrich the conversation. Once shared, leaders and decision-makers can consider issues in the light of all perspectives and engage with each one respectfully, without attachment to personal ownership. Disagreement is welcomed as part of the search for truth, provided it's expressed with civility and deep respect for the humanity and dignity of others. No voice is dismissed, and no contribution is belittled.

In his current role, Monfils works to embed principle-based approaches into the organizational culture. He has introduced guiding principles that reinforce positive corporate values and provide a framework for making decisions rooted in justice and fairness. This means establishing a clear, values-driven foundation for decision-making—one where choices are not dictated by short-term gains, personal biases, or hierarchical pressures but rather by ethical considerations, long-term impact, and a commitment to truth and integrity. Although these principles can sometimes initially face resistance, Monfils observed that, over time, they began to shape the organizational culture, even as challenges arose when these principles were not fully supported by executive leadership.

He acknowledged that shifting organizational culture like this can be challenging. As he put it, organizations face a lot of turbulence as they evolve, particularly when balancing profit-driven goals with a commitment to principles and values. Although profitability is essential for sustainability and growth, it becomes problematic when pursued at the expense of fairness, accountability, and long-term ethical considerations. Monfils highlighted that making this shift requires discipline, practice, and a shared commitment to integrity. For Monfils, this process of cultural evolution represents a microcosm of the broader forces of integration and disintegration at play in society.

"We tend to live separate lives," he said. "But the more you can bridge the gap between your business life, your family life, and your spiritual life, the better."

As a leader, this also meant taking a critical look at himself and making sure that he acts, speaks, and makes decisions based on the greater good—not just on his own narrow interests. When Monfils first came on board at Amazon, he was entrusted with significant responsibility by a mentor. He recognized the importance of humility, especially when faced with high-stakes responsibilities, emphasizing that ego can be a destructive force that contributes to disintegration. He explained that genuine leadership requires setting aside self-interest in order to cultivate unity within teams and organizations while becoming a clear channel for guidance. He views his role as an opportunity to rise to the trust placed in him, guided by principles and a desire to serve the greater good.

Overall, Monfils underscored the importance of building organizations that operate not on outdated, opportunistic models but on a foundation of principles that cultivate empathy and cohesion. To do this, he believes that leaders must maintain the highest intentions, recognizing their role as guides in fostering a culture of fairness, accountability, and purpose.

By integrating these qualities into organizations, we can counter the forces of disintegration and move toward a more unified and just way of working and living. The journey from chaos to coherence mirrors these twin forces of disintegration and integration, as the unraveling of outdated structures gives way to the emergence of new, more harmonious patterns. Both processes of disintegration and integration require deep reflection, adaptation, and the conscious cultivation of unity amid disruption, both internally and externally.

The Power of Presence

Coherence and empathy are not only about structural alignment; they're also about presence. True presence—whether between employer and employee, among friends, or within ourselves—has the power to transform relationships and foster deeper connections.

The power of presence opens a space of authenticity, promotes understanding, and lays the foundation of healthy collaboration. Presence enables us to shift from fear-based, reactive decision-making to purpose-driven leadership. It helps us quiet our mental noise to access deeper intuition and insight, indispensable inner tools when faced with increasing complexity and rapid change.

In the workplace (as in life), being present trains emotional intelligence, improves relationships, deepens empathy, solidifies trust, and allows for more aligned communication. Leaders who model presence create conditions in which new ideas can emerge and innovation can flourish, where workers are appreciated, and where co-owned vision can evolve rather than be imposed.

On an individual level, presence allows us to regain internal balance in times of external turbulence. It reacquaints us with what matters most so that we can move through life with more resilience, equanimity, and grace. When we anchor ourselves in presence, we can connect with higher intentions and allow outdated, egoic fragmentation to dissolve. By rooting into presence, we can better integrate our values and align those to our actions—guiding us from confusion to clarity and from fear to empowered action.

Presence, then, is not simply a quality of self—it's a means of alchemy, a way of traversing from the realm of the disorganized to the organized, from the superficial to the deep, from the transient to the enduring.

Better Together

As Judd Allen explores in his book *Better Together: How to Support the Proactive Mental Health of Family, Friends, and Coworkers*, our ability to move away from chaos and into coherence depends on our willingness to embrace connection—both within ourselves and with others.[20]

Forty-six percent of the US population will experience mental health challenges during their lifetimes.[21] Allen's book provides strategies on how you can help friends, family, and coworkers adopt proactive mental health attitudes and behaviors that result in happier, healthier, and more productive lives. *Better Together* provides a step-by-step approach, solid advice, case studies, checklists, and revealing self-tests that take the guesswork out of peer support.

Here are some key tips that Allen offers for setting proactive mental health goals:

- Identifying excellent role models
- Eliminating barriers to change
- Finding or creating supportive environments
- Avoiding setbacks or working through them
- Celebrating progress and success

By fostering coherence in our personal and professional lives, we can step into the light of unity and purpose, contributing to a future that reflects humanity's highest ideals and shared aspirations. In this journey from chaos to coherence, we find not only hope but also the profound realization that we are, indeed, better together.

From there, we can transform both businesses and industries. Bringing this kind of empathy-based coherence to the organizational or industry level necessitates concrete structural changes. Protocols and processes must prioritize alignment among values, goals, and strategies. These structural changes should be informed by the individual values and voices of each team member, contributing to a shared purpose that serves a greater good.

I leave you with a quotation from a friend of mine, Sovaida Ma'ani, author and founding director of the Center for Peace and Global Governance: "Oneness, justice, and love are not isolated principles but are deeply interconnected. When combined, they create a harmonious framework for ethical decision-making and action and provide a road map to develop the right conditions for ethical organizations to flourish."

As this chapter concludes, I invite you to take a moment to reflect on this quotation from Ma'ani as well as on some of the following questions:

REFLECTION QUESTIONS

- How do you perceive the forces of disintegration and integration unfolding in your personal and professional life? What role do you see yourself playing in this process?
- What steps can you take to align your personal goals and values with the broader purpose of your organization?
- How can you deepen your understanding of the *why* behind your actions and decisions? How might this clarity influence your interactions with others?
- In what ways can consistent communication and feedback loops enhance coherence and empathy in your workplace or community?
- Reflect on a time when true presence transformed a relationship or situation in your life. How can you cultivate more of this presence in your daily interactions?
- What protocols or processes could you implement to foster a culture of coherence and mutual support in your organization?

- How does the metaphor of holding hands resonate with your vision for integration and unity? How can you embody this metaphor in your actions?
- How can you foster deeper connections and a sense of "better together" in your personal and professional spheres?
- In what ways have you helped both individuals and your entire organization improve?
- What impact does your leadership have on those around you?
- What would you consider to be the soul of your company? How can you preserve and strengthen this soul?

CHAPTER 6

Abundance: Leading with Integrity

Do not be satisfied until each one with whom you are concerned is to you as a member of your family. Regard each one either as a father, or as a brother, or as a sister, or as a mother, or as a child. If you can attain to this, your difficulties will vanish, you will know what to do.

—'ABDU'L-BAHÁ

Some may assume that leading with abundance means being traditionally profit-driven. Others may associate that word with manifesting hoards of great personal wealth. As for me, I see the abundance mindset as deeply, inextricably intertwined with integrity, service, and joy. This kind of abundance cannot be reduced to individual gain alone. Enrichment at the expense of others cannot be abundance with integrity.

What *does* it take to lead with abundance and integrity in today's world? The chapter's epigraph attempts to answer this essential question, and it carries with it a powerful story.

More than a century ago, in conversation with an English clergyman, 'Abdu'l-Bahá addressed the stark extremes of wealth and poverty in society. He was profoundly struck by the plight of the destitute, both in rural English villages and in urban London.

In an earnest discussion with a parish rector, he remarked,

> I find England awake; there is spiritual life here. But your poor are so very poor! This should not be. On the one hand, you have wealth and great luxury; on the other, men and women are living in the extremities of hunger and want. This great contrast of life is one of the blots on the civilization of this enlightened age. You must turn attention more earnestly to the betterment of the conditions of the poor.[1]

For me, abundance without integrity is not true wealth or security. Gain that causes others' loss or pain necessarily divides humanity rather than integrating communities—much less seeing all others as members of a shared human family. My process of seeking to lead with both integrity and abundance has been a deeply personal journey, one that has shaped my mission to serve humanity. Through my work and the meaningful conversations I've had with visionary leaders and colleagues, I have deepened my understanding of how spiritual values can be integrated into business and pursued in a spirit of service, elevating both enterprise and society.

Abundance, the third pillar of the HEAL (hope, empathy, abundance, and legacy) framework, is a powerful tool for leading with trust, grace, and integrity. It shifts our perspective from scarcity to possibility. It reminds us that money is another form of energy, one that can either create or destroy. It encourages us to foster environments where respect, compassion, and ethical behavior flourish. By embracing an abundance mindset, leaders can create a culture that celebrates individual strengths, empowers team members, and ultimately drives high performance while maintaining a focus on people-first principles. This approach enhances organizational success while aligning business goals with broader societal and environmental considerations.

The belief in an abundance mindset has also guided my approach as an investor. For most of my career, I've anchored myself in the conviction that investing for both people and the planet is more than just the right thing to do. I think it's an absolutely essential practice that should be accessible to anyone, regardless of their financial means.

My mother once captured the essence of my work in a simple yet profound way. When someone described me as very ambitious, she replied, "Jenna's ambitious to serve the world." Her words have remained a touchstone for me, reminding me to stay true to her perception and challenging myself to define true ambition in terms of impact and service, not just personal gain.

SWEET MEMORIES OF MY MUM AND FAMILY CELEBRATING

Although I'm not able to single-handedly serve the entire world through my personal and professional choices, I know our choices ripple out. I also recognize that we're living in a time of rapid change and urgent need. Those of us in positions to redefine leadership and governance have a unique opportunity to contribute toward a protopian process of building a better world, even as old systems disintegrate.

Meanwhile, many companies struggle with workplace cultures of passiveness and cynicism as well as with growing disillusionment with current forms of leadership. As new challenges arise each day, there's a pressing need for companies to adopt new management practices that foster cultures of learning, collaboration, and trust.

In times of crisis and disruption, many leaders default to cost cutting to preserve profitability. However, the most resilient organizations focus on identifying opportunities, pressure-testing their operations, and making strategic investments to emerge stronger. This requires adopting three critical mindsets: sensemaking in crisis, maintaining a bootstrapping ethic, and balancing the needs of all stakeholders.

What do we mean by leadership integrity? I define having integrity as practicing consistent alignment among what we think, say, and do. Although we all miss the mark at times, as long as we sincerely aim to match our ideals to our actions in business, that is the path of leadership integrity.

At the heart of my philosophical and professional journey is a quotation that has profoundly shaped my worldview: "The remedy the world needeth in its present-day afflictions can never be the same as that which a subsequent age may require. Be anxiously concerned with the needs of the age ye live in, and centre your deliberations on its exigencies and requirements."[2]

This passage was written by Bahá'u'lláh in the *Tabernacle of Unity*. This powerful statement has been a beacon of inspiration and a daily reminder to reflect on my place and role within the complexities of our contemporary world. From an early age, I have been captivated by the intricate dance between the material and spiritual aspects of life, exploring how these dimensions can be harmonized to foster a more equitable and sustainable world.

The Bahá'í International Community recently publicly discussed societal harmony and examined deeper questions about the nature of relationships. In their comments, they highlighted a metaphor from the Bahá'í teachings that compares society to the human body, where diverse yet interconnected parts must work together for the well-being of the whole. They went further to state that it was "the realization that we are all one—that it is not 'us' and 'them.' It is our society we live in. It is our organizations. It is our fellow citizens. And how can we all collaborate or unite in our efforts?"[3]

My career in the impact investing sector has provided a fertile ground for engaging with these themes on a practical level. In this field, discussions often revolve around the challenge of balancing financial returns with the imperative to address social and environmental issues. Another statement from the Bahá'í International Community eloquently captures this tension: "The progress and vitality of humanity requires a coherent relationship between the material and non-material dimensions of human life . . . if wealth is accumulated by the oppression and domination of others, how can we hope to mobilize the material, intellectual, and moral resources needed to eradicate poverty?"[4]

The principles of coherence and integrity both stand out as guiding lights in these reflections. They challenge us to look beyond mere wealth accumulation and consider how this wealth is generated.

This ethos is especially relevant to my work with next-generation family members inheriting wealth. Some of these fortunes were built on industries such as fossil fuels and tobacco—sectors known for their extractive and exploitative practices. Engaging with these next-generation inheritors involves deep, reflective conversations about the origins of their wealth and its implications for their ethical and moral responsibilities moving forward. These discussions often center on reimagining how this capital can be deployed in ways that promote social and environmental healing and progress.

The notion of managing financial affairs with spiritual alignment reiterates integrity as a crucial aspect of a spiritually aligned life. As highlighted by the Universal House of Justice in 2015, "Managing one's financial affairs in accordance with spiritual principles is an indispensable dimension of a life lived coherently. It is a matter of conscience, a way in which commitment to the betterment of the world is translated into practice."[5]

At Impact Experience, my leadership focus has been to prioritize genuine connection by investing deeply in relationships with community members and partners—getting to know their families, stories, and lives beyond the surface. This proactive approach builds trust and lays a strong foundation for meaningful collaboration while minimizing potential conflicts.

In addition to fostering connection, reflective practice is central to this process. It encourages us to examine the impact of our actions and ensure that they align with our values of ethical and sustainable business. More than just talk and navel-gazing, we focus on action-oriented engagement, translating our principles into tangible outcomes that benefit both our organization and society at large. By seeking to embody the change we seek, the goal is to create ripples of transformation that guide businesses toward equitable and inclusive practices.

For example, in Williamson, West Virginia, Impact Experience has partnered with the Williamson Health and Wellness Center to support their work around addressing social determinants of health. West Virginia struggles with the highest rates of diabetes and drug addiction and with one of the highest unemployment rates in the United States.[6] This work has included supporting the expansion of the federally qualified health care clinic, which helped achieve one of the greatest reductions in diabetes rates of a rural community in the country.

Circulating Wealth with Purpose

An exemplary case of leading with integrity and understanding money as a form of energy is Jullien Gordon, the founder and CEO of the Multifamily Movement. His work demonstrates the collective growth and integration we all benefit from when wealth is not merely accumulated but rather circulated for the greater good.

The Multifamily Movement brings together multiple families to access real estate as an asset class and to create what he calls *re-generational wealth*. Initially, the company's goal was to "free" three hundred people from a generational cycle of disadvantage and lack through a movement they call the Above Ground Railroad, in reference to the famous nineteenth-century American escape network. As the Multifamily Movement grew, so did its vision, expanding to a new target of three thousand owners and $1 billion in real estate acquisitions.

In my conversation with Gordon, he shared profound insights into money, leadership, and legacy. He believes that money is stored energy—useless unless put into motion. Whether inherited through generational wealth or earned through business, he sees money as something to be directed toward meaningful causes, investments, and initiatives that advance what he calls God's work—bringing a sense of purpose, justice, abundance, and prosperity to communities. For Gordon, true leadership is about using money as a current of energy that flows into businesses, institutions, and individuals who are working to uplift society.

"Money is called currency for a reason," he explained. "It's supposed to have a current. The goal is not accumulation but circulation. Just like a river has a current, money must move to create impact. If wealth remains stagnant—like a dammed river—it loses its potential. The real winners in life are not those who hoard the most money but those who circulate the most good." Elizabeth Husserl explores similar ideas in her book *The Power of Enough*, where she examines the spiritual and psychological freedom that comes from redefining wealth beyond accumulation. One of her key insights is that when we align our relationship to money with a sense of sufficiency rather than scarcity, we unlock a deeper flow of generosity, creativity, and collective well-being.

Gordon puts this philosophy into practice through his real estate work. He owns and manages quality affordable housing for approximately seventy people—many of them single mothers and children—in Brooklyn, Oakland, New Orleans, and Atlanta. His approach prioritizes dignity and care: ensuring that maintenance issues are addressed immediately, working with tenants who struggle with payments, and even waiving rent during times of crisis.

"Eviction is the last thing I want to do," he emphasized. "I work with my tenants, not against them. During times of abundance, I have chosen to forgo collecting rent from tenants experiencing hardship, especially during the holiday season. This is how I apply spiritual principles in my business—by leading with integrity, compassion, and service."

Jullien Gordon's work is a testament to how money, when viewed as energy, can be channeled to create lasting impact. Through his leadership, he helps individuals build wealth while also redefining the role of business and investment in service to humanity. His approach to re-generational wealth ensures that prosperity is not just about financial success but about leaving the world better than we found it—one investment, one home, and one act of integrity at a time.

Operationalizing Moral Excellence and Love in Business

According to a 2018 study published in *Frontiers of Psychology*, leaders who exhibit strong ethical values demonstrably build more trust with their teams, foster a more positive organizational culture, and inspire more ethical behavior from others.[7]

How can we move from a culture of mere compliance to a culture of active moral excellence? For that we need leadership that leads by example. The question is this: *How can we infuse values into the fabric of the culture so that everyone can demonstrate responsibility?*

When thinking about how I can best model this values-driven culture, I often reground in the following quotation from the Bahá'í writings: "Let your heart burn with loving kindness for all who may cross your path."

In business, this spirit of loving-kindness looks like integrity and the spirit of service that builds real trust. Such trust speeds up responsible decision-making, problem-solving, conflict management, and strategic planning. It develops character, integrity, leadership, and lasting personal and professional relationships. In fact, trust is one factor that provides the unquestionable foundation on which everything else in an organization is built.

But we still often lack the know-how by which we can consistently operationalize this seemingly simple yet very complex and profound concept in our organizations. For this and other reasons, trust was identified by Mehran Ferdowsian, founder of the 9-Core

Competencies and professor of management at Wilkes University, as among the nine strategic competencies[8] that organizations need to differentiate themselves from their competitors, develop a sustained competitive advantage, and add meaningful value to the work and lives of the people around them and to society at large. This solid foundation of trust serves as the bedrock for all other core competencies.

Leaders can ask themselves the following question: *How can I fully operationalize and institutionalize ethics as well as a sense of responsibility throughout the entire organization?* The answer begins within, with leaders acting as role models to exemplify and *live* those qualities and values they wish to see in others.

Decision-Making in a Context of Moral Excellence

What is the anatomy of a good and responsible, strategic decision in a culture of moral excellence? To get a sense of the overall structure of such decision-making, we must first understand what we mean by the words *good, responsible,* and *strategic.*

A good decision is one that listens—that gathers in all that it can hear, not only from data and markets, but from the deeper voices of conscience and community. It is a choice that honors moral insight as carefully as financial return, recognizing that integrity, too, is a form of value. To decide well requires humility: to look with clear eyes at the footprint a company has already made, within its walls and upon the wider world. Good decisions grow in sunlight, not shadow. They invite in the perspectives that have been left outside the room, knowing that wisdom becomes whole only when many voices are heard. To understand whether a decision is truly good, we might ask: *Does it bring the parts of our work into harmony with the whole? Does it create a path where competing interests can find balance, guided always by the purpose that first called the organization into being?*

A *responsible* decision is one that is likely to meet the organization's goals without creating attendant problems. In a culture of moral excellence and abundance, we broaden the understanding of stakeholders' typical management at the board level to one that encompasses both employees and community members. It may also involve reflection on a set of values that the organization has committed to—for instance, environmental impact. For our purposes, responsibility is not narrowly defined as the financial bottom line but rather more broadly to include *how* that aspirational bottom line gets achieved—namely, in a manner consistent with the organization's stated values.

Finally, a decision is *strategic* when it is based on information that gives us answers to such questions as these: *Where are we now? How do we get to where we want to go?* For strategic decisions, we consider the status and available resources of the organization, then apply all of this information to get ever closer to where the organization wants to go.

Integrity and Abundance in Action

Leading with integrity and abundance is all about examining our individual ethics to foster positive change. For Miriam Rivera, CEO, cofounder, and managing director of the venture capital firm Ulu Ventures, this has everything to do with inclusion and diversity in leadership.

According to Rivera, inclusive leadership drives innovation, creativity, and stronger decision-making by bringing together diverse viewpoints and lived experiences. This in turn leads to more ethical business practices, more holistic problem-solving, and ultimately, a more just and equitable society.

Rivera is a dear friend, and I had the opportunity to interview her onstage at the twenty-fifth anniversary celebration for the Center for Social Innovation at the Stanford Graduate School of Business as well as for this book.

Rivera's firm, Ulu Ventures, is a top-tier seed-stage venture capital firm based in Silicon Valley and focused on investing in high-growth and market-leading technology companies. Ulu's investment thesis is based on the concept that diversity is profitable, coupled with a data-driven, repeatable process for making investment decisions. More than 80 percent of Ulu portfolio companies are founded by diverse teams. The firm has over $400 million in assets under management, including ten unicorns valued at greater than $1 billion. Ulu was the first Latina-led venture fund in Silicon Valley, and Rivera is a recognized pioneer in both the tech and the Latinx communities. Before cofounding Ulu, Rivera had served since 2001 as vice president and deputy general counsel at Google. Her work to simplify contracts helped Google scale from $85 million to $10 billion in just five years. Rivera has also served on the board of trustees at Stanford University and on the board of Sesame Street.

A 2025 *Wall Street Journal* article noted that Ulu Ventures managed to raise $208 million for its fourth fund from a long list of institutional limited partners committed to the firm's strategy of funding diverse tech founders—even in spite of the 2025 mass corporate retreat from diversity, equity, and inclusion efforts. The firm "stuck with its data-driven approach to filtering out industry biases and investing in a variety of founders—without excluding any group."[9]

In my conversation with Rivera, she shared invaluable insights into how diversity in venture capital can be a powerful force for financial success and social impact. At Ulu Ventures, diversity is not just a talking point; it's a fundamental strategy. Rivera sees venture capital as a strategic instrument to change the economic landscape by altering who starts companies, who gets hired, who gains equity, and ultimately, who accumulates wealth in the US. Given that only 1 percent of American companies successfully raise venture capital (even though these companies account for more than 40 percent of public companies), the impact of more inclusive investing can be profound. By supporting diverse founders and investors, firms such as Ulu Ventures help bridge the wealth gap among different demographics and ensure that solutions for pressing social and economic issues emerge from the communities most affected.

Beyond venture capital, Rivera's own career journey reflects the balance between finance and social impact. As a first-generation college graduate burdened with $130,000 in student loans while also supporting her mother for twenty-eight years, she understood the importance of pursuing work that was both financially viable and meaningful. While building her career as a lawyer and start-up founder, she consistently found ways to serve her community, whether through board positions at domestic abuse shelters or by volunteering at her church and impact-driven organizations.

Another example of Rivera's commitment to aligning financial strategy with social good is her work with Acumen America, an impact venture capital firm that channels philanthropic capital into for-profit technology companies serving low-income Americans. As a longtime member of Acumen's investment committee and board, she has helped refine their investment approach—bridging traditional venture capital methodologies with an impact-first lens. This allowed the firm to apply rigorous decision-making while prioritizing opportunities that traditional investors might overlook.

Even at Ulu Ventures, which is focused on generating strong venture capital returns, Rivera sees a natural overlap with impact. Nearly 50 percent of Ulu's portfolio includes companies working in education, environmental sustainability, financial inclusion, and access to justice. She understands that it may not always be possible to pursue both financial gain and impact in equal measure at every stage of one's career. Still, she said, the skills gained in the for-profit sector can be immensely valuable for mission-driven organizations, and vice versa.

Whether through investing in billion-dollar companies with social impact potential or contributing expertise to nonprofits such as Sesame Street, Rivera embodies the idea that leading with integrity means finding ways to create lasting change—no matter the industry or career path. Rivera believes in servant leadership, where leaders serve the agenda of their team or organization rather than their own, more narrow, interests. She references Jim Collins's level 5 leadership framework, which emphasizes humility and a focus on the needs of others, as instrumental to how she views impactful leadership. Above all, she said that cultivating a positive relationship with yourself creates an inner reservoir of abundance and goodwill from which to give and serve others.

Clint Korver, cofounder and managing director of Ulu Ventures, has reflected on the concept of the red and black letter world, a distinction that was inspired by his work in decision analysis and ethics. The black letter world represents domains where rational analysis, logic, and quantifiable decision-making predominate, while the red letter world encompasses the more intuitive, spiritual, and meaning-driven aspects of life. Korver has suggested that although much of professional life emphasizes the black letter approach, most of life is ultimately lived in the red letter world, where intuition, values, and deeper purpose matter most. This viewpoint emphasizes that humans are spiritual beings navigating a fundamentally human experience, echoing ideas from philosophers such as Pierre Teilhard de Chardin.

By framing life through this lens, Korver shows that the red and black letter worlds are not in opposition but rather in dialogue, creating a more integrated path toward abundance. Abundance arises when we honor both dimensions—the clarity and rigor of rational analysis alongside the richness of intuition and spirit. In business, relationships, and personal growth, abundance is not merely defined by material gain but also by the flourishing that comes from aligning decisions with deeper meaning. Recognizing that logic and intuition together can guide us toward choices that expand possibility rather than restrict it allows for a more generative view of success and fulfillment.

Voices of Integrity: Wisdom from Leaders Who Inspire Change

In the countless interviews I've conducted with visionary leaders and agents of change, I have encountered leadership and integrity that leave a profound impact. One such leader is Fletcher Harper, executive director of GreenFaith, a global network of people of faith who advocate for green energy progress. Their work is driven by a deep commitment to both diverse religious faiths and environmental justice. In my conversation with Harper, he shared the motivations that shaped his journey from his ordination as an Episcopal priest in 1992, after attending Union Theological Seminary, to his tenure as a chaplain and rector in northern New Jersey. Although his early work was rooted in parish leadership, he felt something was missing—a stronger connection between faith and environmental responsibility.

"I believed then, as I do now, that religious institutions play an important role in shaping the moral and spiritual character of individuals and society," Fletcher explained. "Yet, in my work in a parish, I felt there was a gap. My love for the environment had always been strong, but I found it challenging to connect faith with environmental responsibility. Resources to bridge this divide seemed scarce, and many people of faith struggled to see the ethical and spiritual dimensions of environmental issues."

That changed when he discovered GreenFaith, an organization dedicated to educating clergy and lay leaders about the connection among sacred texts, theological traditions, and environmental stewardship. GreenFaith empowers religious institutions to operate sustainably, serve as models for their communities, and advocate for environmental justice, particularly for society's most vulnerable populations.

Beyond his environmental mission, Harper shared profound insights into leadership and organizational development, particularly regarding the balance between staying true to one's core values and allowing space for others to grow. For him, integrity in leadership starts with clarity of purpose.

"The key," he said, "is undertaking a process of becoming clear about your core values—your most cherished beliefs—and never violating them. If that means your career or organization evolves in an unexpected direction, so be it. If those beliefs are truly tested and remain true for you, they should guide your decisions."

As an executive director, Harper has learned that leadership is not about dictating outcomes but about fostering an inclusive, values-driven culture. Although he brings experience and deeply held convictions, he understands that his role is to share insights in a way that influences rather than commands.

"Letting go as a leader doesn't mean stepping away entirely; it means shifting your focus from controlling outcomes to creating a system that allows others to discover and articulate their own beliefs," he said. "The challenge is to maintain progress in the organization while also fostering an environment where team members feel empowered to develop their own leadership."

Another inspiring leader I spoke with who embodies integrity and abundance is Jason Yotopoulos, CEO of Emerald Gate. Yotopoulos leads with a vision that intertwines scientific discovery, personal transformation, and social impact. Through his Emerald Gate Foundation, he supports research that focuses on expanding human consciousness, improving the human condition, and addressing real-world challenges. In particular, it focuses on research into the interaction among conscious human intention, subtle energy, and biology to promote healing and well-being while also applying innovative social and economic models to empower local communities.

In our conversation, Yotopoulos shared that some of the most successful investors he knows—those who remain grounded and make decisions with clarity, even in turbulent markets—often have a deep spiritual practice. These individuals operate from a heightened sense of intuition, making choices not out of fear or ego but from a place of integrity, abundance, and alignment with a greater purpose. He sees this ability to step outside of oneself and tune into a deeper wisdom as a common thread among leaders who create lasting impact.

Beyond financial success, Yotopoulos has observed that many high-net-worth individuals ultimately shift their focus from wealth accumulation to a more profound question related to abundance: *What do I do with this wealth to make a difference?*

This shift often arises from personal hardship, deep disillusionment, or an existential realization that material success alone does not bring fulfillment. For many, this turning point sparks a search for legacy, meaning, and contribution. Yotopoulos believes that true success comes from having a North Star—a purpose that transcends financial gain and serves a higher calling. Whether in business or in life, he emphasizes the importance of intentionality and personal excitement in one's pursuits. For him, and for many others leading with integrity, success is not just about profit but about aligning with values, pursuing work that resonates deeply, and using wealth as a tool to create lasting, positive change in the world.

Mark Grovic, a veteran impact investor and founder of New Markets Venture Partners, agrees. Grovic has dedicated his career to aligning business success with social impact, particularly in education and workforce development. With more than thirty years of investment experience and a background as an award-winning professor, Grovic has consistently explored how business models can be designed around service, demonstrating that companies can both solve social problems and generate financial returns.

Whether through volunteerism or as an integral part of one's professional mission, Grovic emphasized that true leadership comes through serving others. He believes that building business models around solving real-world challenges creates a deeper sense of fulfillment and integrity in leadership. For him, a big part of his inspiration is waking up each day with the knowledge that his work contributes to meaningful change. By integrating purpose into business strategy, Grovic exemplifies how leading with integrity is not just about ethics; it's about building sustainable systems that uplift communities while fostering long-term success.

Grovic emphasized the significance of self-love and self-validation in his spiritual approach. For him, infusing love and meaning into one's work and creations aligns with socially responsible investing. In addition to self-love, another important dimension that came up in interviews for this book was the importance of self-knowledge.

There are far too many examples of exemplary impact investors and leaders for me to name here, but let's end with a few more whom I spoke with. Emily Chew, head of sustainability at GIC, an $800 billion sovereign wealth fund in Singapore, emphasized a passage from the Bahá'í writings that states, "True loss is for him whose days have been spent in utter ignorance of his self."[10] In addition to the necessity of self-knowledge, Chew underscores the importance of recognizing the interconnectedness of all things, both seen and unseen, and cultivating a sense of possibility for the future.

Yet another inspiring leader in the impact investing sector, and a dear friend of mine, is the late Lisa Hall. Before she passed, she shared with me the importance of intentionality within investing and always being true to oneself. Throughout her career, whether as the CEO of the Calvert Foundation (now called Calvert Impact Capital), the managing director of Anthos Fund, or the impact chair of Apollo Global Management, she emphasized that impact investing is more than just a financial exercise—it's a reciprocal, relationship-driven process that manifests compassion and caring for the world we live in. She shared in an interview for this book about the importance of cultivating love over hate, both personally and organizationally, as a core spiritual principle that guides leaders and investors who seek to align their values with their actions. She drew on a rich tapestry of spiritual insights, including those from her attendance at a Vatican conference on impact investing, illustrating the growing intersection between faith and finance. Hall highlighted that authentic impact investing moves beyond charity; it's about teaching a community to fish, creating sustainable solutions that honor dignity and foster self-sufficiency rather than dependency.

Despite her courageous battle with illness, Hall remained optimistic and grounded in faith, attributing much of her resilience and quality of life to the spiritual support she received. She reminded those walking a similar path that authenticity—being the same person at work and at home—is fundamental to true happiness and spiritual health. Her reflections on fear as the opposite of love and her assertion that impact investing is an antidote to fear capture the essence of her life and work.

Though Hall has since passed away, her spirit continues to inspire those who seek to weave spirituality, investing, and business into a harmonious call to service, justice, and authentic connection. Her legacy reminds us that the journey toward impact is as much about inner transformation as it is about external outcomes.

Harnessing Emerging Technologies for the Power of Good

When considering the question of integrity and abundance, how does the rapid acceleration of artificial intelligence (AI) factor in? The power and influence of AI technologies present both opportunities and risks, necessitating careful consideration of how they can be adapted and harnessed as a force for good.

Two quotations from Martin Luther King Jr. capture my sentiments on the emerging technologies in our world today:

- "Through our scientific and technological genius, we've made of this world a neighborhood. And now, through our moral and ethical commitment, we must make of it a brotherhood. We must all learn to live together as brothers—or we will all perish together as fools."[11]

- “The great problem facing modern man is that the means by which we live have outdistanced the spiritual ends for which we live.”[12]

In an era increasingly shaped by technological advances, how can we ensure that tools such as AI serve not just productivity but also the deeper, essential need for human connection?

A *Harvard Business Review* article highlighted that innovative technologies such as AI, virtual reality (VR), and collaborative platforms have the potential to humanize the workplace, when applied thoughtfully.[13] AI has powerful applications such as personalized medicine while VR can transcend physical barriers, creating immersive simulated environments for genuine interaction. These tools are not just instruments of efficiency; they can also serve as bridges that connect people across distances, cultures, and hierarchies.[14]

However, technology alone cannot foster authentic human connections. Without a strong ethical foundation, these tools risk becoming instruments of surveillance, exclusion, or disconnection. The critical question for values-driven leaders is this: *How can we ensure that emerging technologies are designed and implemented with human nobility and justice at their core?*

This is where values-driven leadership comes in. As a member of Ethical Business Building the Future, a Bahá’í-inspired global community dedicated to applying ethical values in business, I have explored how principles such as justice, equity, and unity can shape the future of my investments. Daniel Truran, founder of Ethical Business Building the Future, talks about how data and key performance indicators alone are insufficient to drive change. Instead, he said, leaders need a compelling narrative rooted in broader systems thinking to shift mindsets toward more impact-driven choices when implementing new technology.

If we can start asking and answering the questions posed next, leaders have the opportunity to guide the integration of technology in ways that do the following:

- **Build inclusivity:** Are we using AI to reduce unconscious bias in hiring and promotions?
- **Foster belonging:** Can collaborative platforms ensure that every voice is heard, regardless of location or rank?
- **Promote well-being:** How are we leveraging technology to support mental health and work-life harmony?[15]

Moving from Adoption to Transformation with AI

It's not enough to simply adopt new tools; we must also transform workplace cultures to fully integrate these innovations into the fabric of human-centric, purpose-driven organizations. Some organizations already use VR to create empathy-building simulations that help employees understand diverse perspectives. For example, Stanford's Virtual Human Interaction Lab uses immersive VR experiences to increase empathy by allowing participants to step into the shoes of others facing challenging life situations, such as homelessness.

Stanford's research shows that participants who experienced the "Becoming Homeless" VR simulation demonstrated significantly greater and longer-lasting empathy compared to those who engaged with traditional media, with 82 to 85 percent of VR participants signing petitions supporting affordable housing versus only about 63 to 67 percent of those who read or viewed non-VR narratives. The lab's work highlights VR as a powerful tool not just for transient emotional impact but for sustained prosocial attitudes and behaviors related to social issues.[16] After coming out of the VR empathy simulations, people practice empathy more in real life.

This resonates deeply with my belief that investments, businesses, and organizations should be built on foundational principles of equity, unity, abundance, and justice—principles that can guide every step of technological implementation.

The Universal House of Justice stated, "Scientific knowledge . . . helps the members of a community to analyse the physical and social implications of a given technological proposal—say, its environmental impact—and spiritual insight gives rise to moral imperatives that uphold social harmony and that ensure technology serves the common good."[17]

When it comes to AI development, there is still much work to be done, particularly around the importance of prioritizing ethical considerations, recognizing the potential risks for encoded bias in AI, displacement of human workers, and rampant misinformation. Although scientific advancements drive the progress of AI, spiritual and ethical insights demand that these technologies be developed responsibly, ensuring that they enhance human well-being rather than exacerbate inequity. Investors who back responsible AI initiatives are helping to shape an industry that values both innovation and ethical responsibility.

Leading with integrity in the era of artificial intelligence requires a commitment to ensuring that technology serves humanity rather than becoming a tool for exploitation. AI has the potential to either reinforce systemic inequities or advance social and environmental progress. The key lies in how it is designed, implemented, and integrated by ethical leaders.

One powerful example of AI being used for the greater good is ÆRTH, a science-based AI platform dedicated to serving the planet.[18] ÆRTH recognizes that our natural living systems are interconnected and dynamic, yet traditional data and investment models often fail to reflect this complexity. By leveraging

AI, ÆRTH seeks to bridge this gap, creating a more holistic and responsive approach to planetary sustainability. The platform integrates scientific insights with artificial intelligence to provide data-driven solutions that align economic incentives with environmental preservation. This enables continuous learning and predictive environmental modeling, which facilitates better-informed, nature-based solutions and climate adaptation strategies. Rather than using AI for short-term profit maximization, ÆRTH demonstrates how technology can be designed to work in harmony with nature, supporting long-term ecological balance and responsible investment.[19]

Larry Brilliant, renowned epidemiologist and philanthropist, is another example of an ethical AI pioneer. Brilliant serves as CEO of Evity.ai, a company I had the opportunity to invest in. Evity is working to revolutionize health care by combining AI technology with medical expertise. At Evity, Brilliant aims to create a smart, hybrid human-AI platform that transforms health care into a more preventive, precise, and personalized system.

Brilliant's approach to business and technology is deeply influenced by his spiritual journey and humanitarian work. He advocates for committing to a path of finding higher purpose in one's work. This philosophy aligns with his view that companies should strive for the greater good. Brilliant's career exemplifies a unique blend of medical expertise, technological innovation, and humanitarian efforts, demonstrating how spirituality, investing, and business can intersect to create meaningful impact.

Another of Evity.ai's investors is Wisdom Ventures, an early-stage venture capital firm focused on bringing together the worlds of spirituality, investing, and business by investing in tech-enabled well-being. The fund is led by Soren Gordhamer, founder of the Wisdom 2.0 conference, alongside partners with deep expertise in both innovation and mindfulness. Wisdom Ventures backs founders who are developing technologies and platforms that nurture human connection, emotional intelligence, and conscious leadership—prioritizing mission alignment and societal impact as much as financial return. Their vision is rooted in the belief that technology and business should serve humanity, enabling more mindful ways of living, healing, and leading.

AI is also being applied to drive systemic change in the financial sector. During my interview with Daryn Dodson of Illumen Capital, we discussed how AI can be a tool for justice when applied with intention. Dodson emphasized the importance of integrating what he calls *ancestral intelligence* alongside technological advancements. In partnership with Impact Experience, Illumen Capital's investors and fund managers undergo an immersive engagement on the historical roots of systemic inequities—tracing the legacy of slavery, lynching, and present-day mass incarceration as well as their impact on asset management and financial markets today.

Through some of Illumen Capital's investments, AI is being used not only for efficiency but also to identify and address biases. By embedding this understanding into investment strategies, Illumen Capital seeks to find ways that AI will help uncover overlooked opportunities, fostering a more equitable financial ecosystem rather than perpetuating existing disparities. Dodson made it clear that although achieving strong financial returns (or alpha)[20] is a goal, it should never come at the expense of humanity. He highlighted that capitalism has been built on exploitative systems and that our current age of rapid change presents an opportunity to redefine success—leveraging AI to build inclusive enterprises that recognize the full potential of all individuals.

Miriam Rivera also shared her experiences with regard to AI. She sees significant potential for AI to drive positive change, particularly in industries that have historically struggled with efficiency due to high technological costs. Rivera highlighted the role of AI in transforming sectors such as education and health care, where automation and optimization could lead to substantial improvements. For instance, one of Ulu Ventures' portfolio companies, Zum, uses AI to optimize school transportation, reducing reliance on large diesel-fueled buses and moving toward electrification. Given that school transportation represents the largest public transportation system in the US, with over a billion rides per month, AI-driven efficiencies in this space could have profound environmental and financial benefits. Similarly, Rivera sees AI's potential in health care, where applications can alleviate the burden on nurses by improving patient management systems, ultimately enhancing both workflow and patient care outcomes.

Rivera also expresses caution regarding AI's ethical implications, particularly in how bias can be embedded into its algorithms. She recounts attending discussions where boardrooms and decision-makers failed to question the ethical ramifications of AI, even as research demonstrates its potential to perpetuate systemic biases. She cites an example of AI models displaying discriminatory pricing recommendations based on race or gender, underscoring the need for vigilance in how these systems are developed and deployed. Rivera finds it alarming when leaders, founders, and investors overlook these concerns, prioritizing accuracy while failing to recognize bias as a fundamental flaw in AI's decision-making. Although she remains optimistic about AI's transformative possibilities, she stresses the need for greater awareness and accountability to ensure that these advancements serve all communities equitably.

As AI systems are becoming more advanced, people are engaging with AI around deeper spiritual and existential questions. By integrating spirituality and ethical reflection into this emerging technology development, we can positively guide the future trajectory of AI development while deepening our own understanding of the nature of consciousness.

Leading with integrity in the age of AI requires more than just adopting new technologies; it demands a rethinking of how we approach leadership, investment, and systemic change. AI, when applied with ethical rigor, can serve as a catalyst for both environmental and social transformation, by aligning progress with justice and innovation with humanity.

This perspective greatly interests Eric Sapp, president of Public Democracy, who works in the data and disinformation space and who is deeply guided by faith and spirituality. Sapp offered unique perspectives, including his view that data itself can become its own form of spirituality. He views data not just as ones and zeros but as repositories of moments, sensations, and feelings, whether of hope, connection, or a sense of individual agency. In particular, when running a big campaign on climate, Sapp realized the data they were creating also represented moments when individuals felt empowered to take constructive, collaborative steps to promote climate justice. He also pointed out that data is the first asset in human history that is not scarcity-based in its value. Understanding data in this way opens new opportunities in how one engages with it.

Luke Stewart, CEO of Adaptic Health and another investee of mine, similarly applies technology to empower patients and communities for better health outcomes. Stewart's insights offer a compelling perspective on how a personal faith journey can inform and drive business decisions. As a child, Stewart was diagnosed with a rare disease and was not expected to live past the age of five. Stewart credits his recovery to his parents' fervent prayers and deep faith in God. Stewart went on to graduate from Duke University with a full scholarship, studying computer science and running on the track team, followed by an MBA at the Stanford Graduate School of Business. Stewart has since sought out a higher calling than mere moneymaking, leading him to the more meaningful, impact-driven work he currently advances.

These deeper spiritual and ethical considerations necessitate a holistic approach—one that ensures technology is built with integrity and a commitment to the greater well-being of humanity. As we stand on the cusp of unprecedented technological growth, this balance between innovation and ethical consciousness will be critical in shaping AI as a force for good.

Fostering a Thriving, Abundant Community Mindset

True, integrity-based leadership extends beyond individual capability—it's about fostering an environment of trust, unity, abundance, and shared purpose. It requires both intention and action rooted in character and a deep commitment to the well-being of others. Leadership development is not solely about acquiring skills but about cultivating the mindset, values, and relationships that allow individuals and organizations to thrive. This growth happens through continuous learning, action, and reflection. Mistakes are inevitable, but progress comes from consistently striving to build a culture of integrity, abundance, collaboration, and service.

One powerful way to rethink leadership is by viewing a company as a community rather than as just an organization. In a true community, individuals work together with a sense of shared responsibility and higher purpose, promoting trust, collaboration, and innovation. The essence of a company—what one might call its soul—lies in the intangible but vital elements that define its purpose, values, and collective vision. To bring clarity and direction to leadership strategy and operations, start by asking questions such as these: *Why does this company exist? How does it contribute to the greater good?* This approach helps address common workplace challenges such as inefficiency, siloed thinking, and lack of engagement, replacing them with a dynamic culture of ownership and interconnectedness.

An emerging model of leadership that embodies these principles of integrity and abundance is soul-driven leadership, which emphasizes transforming self-interest and isolation into a mindset of connectedness and collective care. Soul.com articulates a four-stage transformation process:[21]

- **Creating a new mindset:** Shifting mindsets to unlock new possibilities and channeling untapped energy into meaningful action.
- **Creating a movement:** Inspiring individuals to connect with their organizations at a deeper level, fostering unity and collaboration.
- **Creating new models:** Developing new structures and ways of working that transform organizations into thriving, purpose-driven communities.
- **Creating meaning:** Elevating organizations to become forces for positive change, inspiring industry-wide transformation.

Community building can also take place on a more personal level. Since I was young, I have been hosting discussion groups at my home, a tradition that has grown more meaningful with time. As the world faces increasing challenges, I believe that creating such spaces for genuine connection and community is more important than ever. By inviting friends and neighbors to come together and share perspectives, I have seen how these simple gatherings can foster empathy, understanding, abundance, and a sense of belonging. Anyone can replicate this in their own home. In such a divided world, having a space to assemble and engage in meaningful conversations can be a powerful antidote to isolation and a reminder of our shared humanity.

As you reflect on the insights from this chapter, I invite you to take a moment to assess your own leadership integrity and approach to abundance. Grab a pen and paper and thoughtfully explore the following questions. Allow yourself the time to dive deep into reflection and remember that integrating integrity and abundance into leadership is an ongoing process. Revisit these questions periodically to continue your growth as a values-driven leader.

REFLECTION QUESTIONS

- Are your actions consistent with your beliefs and core values?
- Do you accept responsibility for your mistakes?
- Are you honest with yourself about how your actions might affect others?
- What principles and values define the way that you and your team relate and work together?
- Do you follow through on your commitments and promises?
- Do you act in ways that build trust?
- What opportunities are you aligning with that serve people and the planet and not just profits?
- Are you embedding ethical AI and technological innovation that enhances human dignity and societal well-being?
- Are you reimagining investing and business not as a zero-sum game but as a system where companies thrive by fostering collaboration, sustainability, and inclusivity?
- Are you balancing innovation, growth, and business practices with inclusivity, prosperity, and purpose?
- How can you cultivate a more abundant mindset and approach?

CHAPTER 7

Legacy: From Milestones to Tombstones

What you leave behind is not what is engraved in stone monuments, but what is woven into the lives of others.

—**PERICLES**, A LEADING ATHENIAN STATESMAN AND ORATOR

English theologian and former vice president of the Jesuit institution Heythrop College, Dr. Peter Vardy made the striking choice to keep a coffin—his own—in his office, ever on display as he counseled students and other faculty. His visitors would necessarily confront this symbol of mortality during their meetings, a physical reminder that our time is finite and that our choices matter. This practice, although unconventional, serves as a powerful prompt for students to consider their lives' direction and purpose.

As we near the end of this book exploring the intersection of spirituality, investing, and business, we come to the final pillar of the HEAL (hope, empathy, abundance, and legacy) framework: legacy. The contemplation of our own mortality has long served as a powerful catalyst for transformation in how we live, work, and invest. When we pause to consider our finite existence in this world, the veil between the material and the spiritual realms often feels more translucent, revealing profound truths about what truly matters in our lives.

Although it might seem to be the ultimate end point, death can paradoxically serve as our greatest teacher about life. This wisdom emerges across cultures and traditions, from the Buddhist practice of *maraṇasati* (mindfulness of death) to the Latin phrase *memento mori* ("remember that you must die"). These practices are not meant to invoke fear or paralysis but rather to inspire intentional living and conscious decision-making.

Personal encounters with death often provide the most profound lessons. I was present for the passing of my mother and my grandmother, both of which illuminated the mysterious threshold between worlds. In fact, my mother's final words were "Frightening but beautiful," which capture the paradoxical nature of death's ability to inspire both awe and anxiety, fear and fascination.

Other modern academics have similarly begun incorporating death awareness exercises in surprising ways. For example, Dr. Roderick Kramer, a professor of psychology at the Stanford Graduate School of Business, teaches a course called Lives of Consequence that I had the opportunity to take. As part of the syllabus requirements, he asks each student to write their own obituary. I found this a powerful exercise to really tune into what legacy I am seeking to leave.

Stephen Covey, the author of *7 Habits of Highly Effective People*, similarly promotes a principle of beginning with the end in mind to encourage reflection on mortality. Such practices help bridge the gap between our current actions and our desired legacies.

Calvin Mackie, a mentor, educator, and entrepreneur, embodies the principle of reflecting on legacy through his dedication to empowering young people in his local New Orleans communities to pursue fields in science, technology, engineering, and mathematics through his work with STEM NOLA. By keeping in mind how his impact will outlive his actions, Mackie demonstrates how one's work can extend far beyond personal success to uplift entire communities.

When reflecting on legacy, Elizabeth Garlow, a fellow at the think tank New America, considers the importance of building a more beloved community through our actions in business and investing. Her focus has been on reimagining economic systems through a lens of faith and spirituality. Drawing inspiration from the late Pope Francis, Garlow emphasizes that "the most important intervention of our times is a cultural intervention. Rather than a technocratic fix, we have to fundamentally shift the culture."

In an interview for this book, Garlow shared that how wealth is accumulated is just as important as the ends to which that wealth is directed. She shared the example of ShoreBank and how groups of Catholic women pioneered financial services for those historically shut out of the system. Their work helped give birth to the broader Community Development Financial Institution movement, which has been instrumental in unlocking capital into overlooked communities.

At the heart of this rethinking is a deeper question about risk. Traditionally, finance has treated risk as a matter of returns and default, but Garlow presses us to ask instead, What is the risk of *not* having a livable future? This reframing places long-term human and ecological well-being at the center of economic decision-making.

Her reflections also resonate with the late Pope Francis's call to pay attention to God's economy, one that asks us not only how much we can accumulate but also what is *enough*. From this perspective, genuine wealth emerges not from surplus capital but from relationships. Garlow notes that the very place of our woundedness can become the place of our greatest blessing, inviting us to see interdependence as the foundation of any lasting prosperity.

The etymology of investing—from the Latin *investire*, meaning "to clothe"—reminds us that to invest is not simply to allocate capital but to wrap our resources around what we hold most dear. Just as the garments we choose both protect us and signal who we are, our investments reveal our priorities and shape the identity we project into the world. And like clothing passed down through generations, these choices become part of the fabric of our legacy, carrying forward the values we choose to embody and extend beyond our own lifetime.

When we embrace death awareness, we find ourselves naturally drawn toward more meaningful deployment of our time, talent, and treasure. Constance Broz, cofounder of Live Earth Farm and an experienced investor, highlighted the importance of finding pleasure in the journey and process and not solely focusing on the end product and outcome.

To help her and her team take a more spiritual approach, she often reflects on the following inquiry: *What questions aren't we asking?* This deceivingly simple reflection enables us to challenge our assumptions and uncover blind spots. Broz believes that everything in the universe is interrelated and that profound insights emerge when engaging from this reality. She draws on the metaphor of convergence, such as where the ocean meets the river—a dynamic and fertile intersection that sustains life and growth. This view invites us to broaden our relationships and embrace multiple perspectives, recognizing that our investments and actions are part of a larger ecosystem of relationships that extend through time and generations.

Broz also emphasizes the role of legacy within this interrelatedness, comparing what we leave behind to how we cultivate soil for future harvests. “Capital for me is very similar to land,” she said in our interview. “It’s something that you need to cultivate and invest in for the long term, considering not just what we need today but what fertile ground we leave for the next generation.”

Broz’s approach to legacy isn’t focused on fixed outcomes but on ongoing relationships and conversations across generations, recognizing that wisdom and vision flow both ways between elders and youth. She suggests that by continuously asking what questions are not being asked, we maintain a posture of curiosity and openness that sustains resilience and deepens meaning—not only in investing but also in the shared human endeavor to contribute to a legacy that transcends individual lifetimes.

Samir Goel, co-CEO of Esusu, a fintech start-up dedicated to promoting financial inclusion, also provides a compelling example of integrating a moral code within business strategy. Goel demonstrates that aligning business practices with ethical considerations can foster positive societal impacts while infusing trillions of dollars into underserved communities.

As a current investor in Esusu, I have been inspired by their approach, which Goel refers to as justice capitalism, a reimagined economic system in which leaders, investors, founders, and workers alike think about how each aspect of their business impacts every member of society. Goel emphasizes the importance of codifying values into the organizational structure. He and his team developed an Esusu Credo that functions as the company’s constitution, encapsulating their mission, vision, values, and operating principles.

Related to the concept of justice capitalism, Dr. Rebecca Henderson, an economist and Harvard Business School professor, has advanced important work on reimagining capitalism by exploring how organizations can be a force for good. Henderson’s work highlights that many individuals who initiate efforts for positive change are often deeply spiritual, drawing on their own traditions as inspiration for their work. Henderson emphasizes that the only way out of our current challenges is by going more deeply within.

In reflecting on legacy, one of the most powerful tools to tap into is intuition. Hrund Gunnsteinsdottir, Icelandic author of *InnSaei: Heal, Revive, and Reset with the Icelandic Art of Intuition,*[1] emphasizes the importance of her culture's conception of intuition. The Icelandic term *innsaei,* often translated to *intuition,* literally means "the sea within." This poetic term underscores the ever-changing and flowing unconsciousness inside us all. Gunnsteinsdottir's reflections on the role of intuition in personal and professional life highlights the necessity of integrating both rational analysis and intuitive understanding into decision-making. My conversations with Gunnsteinsdottir provided an exciting opportunity to learn about this Icelandic conception of intuition.

As Gunnsteinsdottir said in our interview, "Alignment within yourself is always your strongest inner compass. You can't find your security in something that lies external to you." In this way, cultivating intuition can help direct your life toward your values, which paves the way for a legacy also aligned with these values.

Inspired by Gunnsteinsdottir's insights, let's take a fresh look at intuition, recognizing its fundamental role in reason, analysis, and creativity—rather than dismissing it as irrational woo-woo fluff. Approaching intuition with fresh eyes highlights the interconnectedness of individual and collective well-being. Gunnsteinsdottir emphasized the power of focused consciousness through the practice of mindful attention, documenting thoughts in a journal without judgment and identifying recurring patterns. By becoming more conscious of how we think and talk, she believes we share and cocreate the broader culture.

Sara Blakely, founder of Spanx, is also a big advocate for the power of trusting one's intuition. As she put it, "Stay true to yourself and your vision. Don't let any outside force or situation take you off your course." If we can keep this vision in our focus, we can live a life we are proud of and leave behind a legacy that honors that vision.

Benjamin "Benji" Fernandes is a Tanzanian entrepreneur and founder of NALA, a fintech company transforming cross-border payments for emerging markets. Raised in Tanzania, he earned scholarships that brought him to the US at seventeen as the youngest African student admitted to the Stanford Graduate School of Business, where he earned his MBA and was my classmate. He also previously was a national TV personality and worked at the Bill and Melinda Gates Foundation before founding NALA in 2018. Now, under Fernandes's leadership, NALA operates in twenty-one countries. The company, backed by top US investors, empowers millions with accessible financial tools.

Fernandes openly identifies as a person of faith, drawing on spiritual principles such as Romans 12:2: "Do not conform to the pattern of this world, but be transformed by the renewing of your mind. Then you will be able to test and approve what God's will is—his good, pleasing and perfect will." This biblical passage inspires transformation and renewal as a foundation of leadership. This perspective also shapes NALA's mission not only to provide fintech services but also to empower communities, grounded in the conviction that business should be both impactful and principled. Fernandes leads with a legacy mindset, aiming to tackle systemic financial exclusion by providing tools that unlock economic opportunity. He believes that empowering individuals sustainably fosters long-term development, and this conviction deeply informs his leadership approach. Throughout NALA's journey, Fernandes credits faith and discipline for sustaining his vision and resilience. He reframes setbacks as growth and service opportunities, contributing to a legacy of perseverance and purpose. Fernandes embeds his faith in NALA, which I have had the opportunity to invest in, through values of integrity and service. His focus on fostering personal growth and community impact supports a culture built to outlast the founder and create enduring positive change.

For me, one of the most memorable insights into mortality came when I signed up for the transformative Art of Leadership program led by leadership coach Robert Gass. There we were guided through the process of contemplating our own mortality. We were asked to imagine that we had each just been told that we had only one year left to live.

When I sat with that idea, I felt a deep shift in my consciousness. The intuitive exercise stripped away the superficial concerns that often cloud our judgment, bringing into sharp focus what truly matters. This powerful moment of reflection not only heightened my awareness of the finite nature of our existence but also illuminated the interconnectedness of my spiritual path and my role as a leader in the business world.

Overall, it became clear that aligning my investments and business practices with my deepest values was not just a choice but a responsibility—a way to leave a meaningful legacy beyond material success. The meditation on death paradoxically breathed new life into my approach to leadership, inspiring me to foster a more compassionate, purpose-driven environment in my professional endeavors.

Seven Generations

An Indigenous framework that profoundly shapes how many people approach legacy is the concept of the seven generations. This principle urges us to consider the impacts of our decisions not just on the present moment but also on seven generations into the future and to consider the legacy from seven generations in the past as well. This worldview calls for a long-term stewardship mindset deeply rooted in responsibility, care, and interconnectedness. It challenges the short-term thinking so often embedded in conventional business and investing, inviting instead a time horizon that honors ancestors and descendants alike.

During a transformative journey to the Amazon in August 2025 with the Pachamama Alliance, I had the privilege to spend time with the Indigenous Achuar and Sapara communities, whose ways of relating to the rainforest are grounded in this very ethos. Their perspective on preserving the Amazon is inseparable from the spiritual and ecological well-being of all future generations. This sacred commitment to stewardship embodies a holistic approach where protecting the forest is caring for life itself, ensuring the survival and thriving of countless generations to come. These experiences underscored for me that spirituality, environmental preservation, and investment must be woven together with deep respect for intergenerational stewardship. The community and Pachamama Alliance's call to us was to change the dream of the modern world from one that extracts from nature to one that embraces it and protects it as one of the most important ingredients for life on Planet Earth.

Dr. Vian Sharif, a pioneering sustainability expert and transformative leader in innovative environmental technologies, echoes this vision in the business world. As the head of sustainability at FNZ and founder of Nature Alpha, Sharif champions sustainable capital allocation strategies that draw directly from Indigenous wisdom—particularly the seven generations principle—to guide more ethical and far-reaching impact decisions. By reengaging with this ancient yet urgently relevant thinking, Sharif argues that businesses and investors can unlock new pathways to value creation, where ecological integrity and long-term human flourishing are seen as inseparable goals. This reorientation toward the future forces us to confront blind spots in current frameworks and to reimagine investment as a form of ongoing care that transcends immediate profit and that embraces the legacy of life itself.

I chose to close this book by reflecting on the seven generations principle because it offers a profound throughline for the intersection of spirituality, investing, and business explored in these pages. Rooted in Indigenous wisdom, the idea calls on each decision-maker to consider the impact of their actions not only on present stakeholders but also on our great-grandchildren's great-grandchildren—seven generations into the future. This long view of stewardship asks businesses and investors to transcend mere accountability and embrace a deeper sense of personal and collective responsibility. When capital allocation, strategic planning, and organizational culture all begin with the question, *Will this sustain and nourish life far beyond our own time?*, the purpose and power of investing are transformed. Ultimately, the merging of profit, purpose, and profound responsibility sets a new standard, one where abundance is measured not just in material wealth but in enduring ecological integrity and in the flourishing of all communities—present and future. In choosing to act with this vision, business and investment become acts of spiritual care, weaving legacy into the fabric of commerce and ensuring that the world we leave behind is one of possibility for generations yet to come.

REFLECTION QUESTIONS

- If you were to write your tombstone epitaph today, what would it say? What might you want it to say instead?
- Likewise, how would you write your own obituary? What impact would you like to have made?
- How might regular contemplation of your mortality change your current investment decisions and business practices?
- Think of a personal encounter with death or loss. How did that experience influence your perspective on what matters most in life?
- In what ways could your business or organization better integrate awareness of finite time and resources into its decision-making processes?
- How can you better align your daily actions with the legacy you hope to leave behind?
- What spiritual or philosophical practices could you incorporate into your professional life to maintain awareness of what truly matters?

CONCLUSION

Living Your Best Connected Life

As we conclude this exploration of the intersection of spirituality, investing, and business, the HEAL—hope, empathy, abundance, and legacy—framework serves as a guiding light for navigating this profound convergence. Each element of HEAL is not merely a concept but also an applied, ongoing practice, a call to action that invites us to reimagine how we approach wealth, purpose, and connection.

Hope reminds us that every challenge holds the seed of transformation. It embodies the belief in possibilities yet unseen, which fuels resilience and innovation. In investing and in business, hope inspires us to pursue ventures that uplift communities and that create lasting impact, transcending purely short-term gains.

Empathy bridges the gap between profit and purpose. By stepping into the shoes of others—whether clients, colleagues, or communities—we cultivate businesses that are not only successful but also deeply human and mutually beneficial. Empathy transforms transactions into relationships and fosters environments where everyone can thrive.

Abundance shifts our perspective from scarcity to possibility. It challenges us to see resources as tools for shared prosperity rather than as individual accumulation. When an abundance mindset rooted in integrity and a sense of social interconnection guides our decisions, we unlock opportunities to invest in sustainable growth and equitable futures.

Legacy anchors our actions in a vision that extends beyond ourselves. It asks us to consider what we leave behind—not just in material wealth but also in terms of values, relationships, and beneficial systems that endure. Leading with legacy in mind can transform business into a vehicle for spiritual alignment and societal betterment.

As business leaders, founders, and investors, we have an opportunity to engage with money as medicine. For example, for Jullien Gordon, money is not about personal gain but about impact. Whether through paying employees, investing in meaningful ventures, or directly supporting those in need, he believes that the true measure of success is not how much money one accumulates but how much positive change one generates.

"The real winners in this world are not the ones who die with the biggest bank account but those who leave behind the greatest legacy of service, leadership, and ethical values," Gordon said. "How you show up as a business owner, an investor, or an employer—how you embody integrity and purpose—is what ultimately matters."

Lynne Twist, a friend of mine, is the author of *The Soul of Money: Transforming Your Relationship with Money and Life*.[1] Twist, alongside Bill Twist and Sara Vetter, organized the Pachamama Alliance trip I recently attended. Lynne Twist's profound insights reveal how the mindset and beliefs we hold about money deeply influence not only our financial behaviors but also our spiritual and emotional well-being. Drawing on decades of experience working with communities in need and with individuals of wealth, she challenges the prevalent scarcity mentality—a belief that there is never enough—and instead advocates for embracing a sufficiency mindset. This shift encourages recognizing and appreciating when we have enough rather than perpetually chasing more, which enables alignment with one's deepest values and cultivates a sense of abundance grounded in gratitude.

At the heart of Twist's work is the understanding that money itself is neutral—a tool reflecting our intentions and values. When consciously approached as such, money becomes an ally for positive change, fostering generosity, collaboration, and purposeful living. *The Soul of Money* encourages those in business and investing to transform fear-based narratives about wealth into empowering stories that prioritize meaning, social impact, and interconnectedness over simple accumulation.

Her focus on conscious giving and on aligning financial resources with moral and spiritual priorities strongly resonates with impact investing, where capital serves both financial returns and systemic, equitable change. By reconnecting money to purpose, Twist calls on investors and leaders to cultivate a relationship with wealth that embodies stewardship, sufficiency, and service to a larger good. This perspective offers a vital framework for integrating spirituality into investing and business decision-making.

Twist also serves on the board of the Fetzer Institute. Founded by John E. Fetzer, the Fetzer Institute is dedicated to building the spiritual foundation for a loving world by weaving spirituality, science, and social transformation into the fabric of modern organizations and communities. Their work focuses on fostering spiritual innovation, supporting both individual and societal transformation, and on convening thought leaders to explore how ancient wisdom and spiritual practices can be translated for the needs of a rapidly changing world.

Through initiatives such as the Spiritual Innovation Collaborative and multiyear partnerships, Fetzer empowers a new generation of healers, spiritual entrepreneurs, artists, and organizational culture pioneers who are reimagining how the sacred can be embodied across sectors—from philanthropy to democracy to organizational leadership. Their programs emphasize sacred love, belonging, inclusion, and the balance of scientific and spiritual inquiry, aiming to prove that centering the sacred is essential for shared human flourishing and lasting societal impact.

As you step forward from these pages, may the inspiration of these stories and examples, as well as the HEAL framework, serve as both a compass and a catalyst. I hope this book inspires you to build enterprises that harmonize spirituality with strategy, investments with intention, and profits with purpose. Together, through hope, empathy, abundance, and legacy, we can cocreate a world where business is not just a means of economic exchange but also a profound expression of our shared humanity.

The HEAL framework, as well as earlier reflections on optimism, transformation, and resilience, can help us make good, responsible, strategic decisions. Together, these concepts provide a lens for viewing business and a map to help us navigate the intersection of spirituality, investing, and business. In a world where uncertainty creates fear and mental paralysis, we can forge new paths that align purpose with action. Hope fuels vision, empathy fosters inclusivity, abundance drives possibility, and legacy ensures that our impact endures.

As you reflect on your own leadership, investment, or entrepreneurial journey, consider how you can incorporate HEAL in ways that resonate with you. How can you integrate these principles into your work and life? Let this framework be both a guide and an invitation—to lead with integrity, to serve with love, and to leave a legacy that reflects the best of who you are.

ACKNOWLEDGMENTS

This book is the result of a collective journey, and I am deeply grateful to the many people who have walked alongside me in the exploration of how spirituality, investing, and business can align to serve humanity and the planet.

First and foremost, I wish to thank my mother and grandmother for their unwavering love and encouragement. Their grounding presence and constant belief in the possibility of weaving together purpose and practice have sustained me throughout this work.

To my mentors, teachers, dear friends, and spiritual guides: Your wisdom has helped me see that finance, when rooted in compassion and justice, can be a tool for healing and transformation. I am indebted to those who have shown me that the practices of mindfulness and reflection can be powerful companions to capital and commerce.

I also owe deep gratitude to my colleagues and collaborators and to the broader community of impact investors, social entrepreneurs, and spiritually inspired leaders who are redefining what it means to invest with values. The countless conversations, shared experiences, and bold visions contributed by this community continually remind me that business can indeed be a vehicle for service and belonging, without compromising a healthy, growing bottom line.

To my friends and peers who challenged me to think more deeply, question assumptions, and stay true to my values—thank you. Your support gave me courage when doubts arose.

Finally, to all those who are carrying forward the work of building a more just, sustainable, and spiritual economy: This book is for you. May it serve as a resource and an invitation to imagine and act with love, wisdom, and integrity.

Some of the people who have had a profound impact on my life and this book include: Daryn Dodson, Amanda Greco, Rachel Robasciotti, Miriam Rivera, Jacob Harold, Theresa Joseph, Eduardo Briceno, Arabella Napier, Amy Lazarus, Wayne Silby, Rainn Wilson, Lynne Twist, Rob Lalka, Charly Kleissner, Todd Khozein, Luke Stewart, May Samali, Sarah Soule, Jennifer Henderson, Paula Pretlow, Julian MacQueen, Kim MacQueen, Clint Korver, Stephen deBerry, Lisa Hall, Hrund Gunnsteinsdottir, Jennifer Aaker, Sandy Wilkes, Berk Shervin, Shari Slate, and Carla Andrews.

To these individuals and so many others: Thank you. Let's carry on the good work.

ENDNOTES

Introduction

1 Return on impact refers to the positive social and environmental benefits generated by an investment or business activity, considered in addition to traditional financial returns.

2 Baha'u'llah, *The Summons of the Lord of Hosts* (Bahá'í Publishing, 2015), 156.

3 At the time, Mark Carney, the twenty-fourth Canadian prime minister, served as the first non-British governor of the Bank of England and as the United Nations special envoy for climate action and finance.

4 Mark Carney, "Mark Carney on How the Economy Must Yield to Human Values," *The Economist*, April 15, 2020, www.economist.com/by-invitation/2020/04/16/mark-carney-on-how-the-economy-must-yield-to-human-values.

5 Robert F. Kennedy. Address at the University of Kansas. April 18, 1968. Robert F. Kennedy Human Rights. Accessed December 5, 2025. https://rfkhumanrights.org/speech/address-at-university-of-kansas/#:~:text=It%20measures%20neither%20our%20wit,proud%20that%20we%20are%20Americans.

6 Larry Elliott, "Bobby Kennedy Was Right: GDP Is a Poor Measure of a Nation's Health," *The Guardian*, January 17, 2021, www.theguardian.com/business/2021/jan/17/bobby-kennedy-was-right-gdp-is-a-poor-measure-of-a-nations-health.

7 See www.devoted.com.

Chapter 1

1 Dan Byrne, "Board Diversity Leads to Better Profits," Corporate Governance Institute, accessed September 25, 2025, www.thecorporategovernanceinstitute.com/insights/news-analysis/board-diversity-leads-to-better-profits.

2 See www.impact-experience.com.

3 The Bahá'í Faith, "Shoghi Effendi: The Guardian of the Bahá'í Faith," the Bahá'í International Community, 2025, www.bahai.org/shoghi-effendi.

4 Barry-Wehmiller, "Surpassing 100 Acquisitions, Barry-Wehmiller Looks to the Future," February 6, 2018, www.barrywehmiller.com/news/company-news/release/surpassing-100-acquisitions-barry-wehmiller-looks-to-the-future.

5 Brent Stewart, host, *Truly Human Leadership*, podcast, episode 59, "Simon Sinek and Bob Chapman," Barry-Wehmiller, July 20, 2023, www.youtube.com/watch?v=msx-wq8zQagk.

6 Nick Van Dam and Eileen M. Rogers, "People, Purpose, and Performance at Barry-Wehmiller: Business as a Powerful Force for Good," IE Business School, January 2020, https://docs.ie.edu/center-for-corporate-learning-innovation/Business-as-a-Powerful-Force-for-Good.pdf.

7 The Center for Compassion and Altruism Research and Education, "Mission and Vision," Stanford University, 2024, https://ccare.stanford.edu/about/mission-vision.

8 The Dalai Lama Center for Ethics and Transformative Values, "Mission," Massachusetts Institute of Technology, 2025, https://thecenter.mit.edu/home/mission.

9 The Center for Compassion and Altruism Research and Education, "Corporate," Stanford University, 2024, https://ccare.stanford.edu/research/compassion-database/corporate/?utm_source.

10 Dean Hand, Maddie Ulanow, Hongyu Pan, and Kelly Xiao, "Sizing the Impact Investing Market 2024," Global Impact Investing Network, October 23, 2024, https://thegiin.org/publication/research/sizing-the-impact-investing-market-2024.

11 See www.bcorporation.net.

12 Yvon Chouinard, "Earth Is Now Our Only Shareholder," Patagonia, September 14, 2022, www.patagonia.com/ownership.

13 Patagonia Works, "Patagonia's Next Chapter: Earth Is Now Our Only Shareholder," Patagonia, September 14, 2022, www.patagoniaworks.com/press/2022/9/14/patagonias-next-chapter-earth-is-now-our-only-shareholder.

14 Sarah Seward, "15 Examples of Purpose Driven Brands," Wild Wit Design Co., 2025, https://wildwitdesign.com/blog/15-examples-of-purpose-driven-brands.

15 The Bahá'í Faith, Bahá'í Reference Library, "Selections from the Writings of 'Abdu'l-Bahá," The Bahá'í International Community, 2025, www.bahai.org/library/authoritative-texts/abdul-baha/selections-writings-abdul-baha/10#036590639.

Chapter 2

1 Kweilin Ellingrud, Mekala Krishnan, Alexis Krivkovich, et al., "Diverse Employees Are Struggling the Most During COVID-19—Here's How Companies Can Respond," McKinsey & Company, November 17, 2020, https://www.mckinsey.com/featured-insights/diversity-and-inclusion/diverse-employees-are-struggling-the-most-during-covid-19-heres-how-companies-can-respond.

2 Michael Bondar, Roxana Corduneanu, and Natasha Buckley, "Can You Measure Trust Within Your Organization?," Deloitte Insights, February 9, 2022, www2.deloitte.com/us/en/insights/topics/leadership/organizational-trust-measurement.html?utm_source.com.

3 Emma Charlton, "This Is How COVID-19 Has Impacted Workers' Lives Around the World," World Economic Forum, January 4, 2021, www.weforum.org/stories/2021/01/covid-19-work-mental-health-world-economic-forum-ipsos-survey/?utm_source.com.

4 Harvard Medical School, "5 Ways to Hold on to Optimism—and Reap Health Benefits," Harvard Health Publishing, January 20, 2017, www.health.harvard.edu/blog/hold-optimism-reap-health-benefits-2017012011003.

5 Jacqueline Brassey, Aaron De Smet, and Dana Maor, "Developing a Resilient, Adaptable Workforce for an Uncertain Future," McKinsey & Company, December 6, 2024, www.mckinsey.com/capabilities/people-and-organizational-performance/our-insights/developing-a-resilient-adaptable-workforce-for-an-uncertain-future?utm_source.

6 Harvard Medical School, "5 Ways to Hold on to Optimism."

7 See www.illumencapital.com.

8 Jeff Berman, host, *Masters of Scale*, podcast, "How to Raise $172M for the Underinvested, with Stacy Brown-Philpot," June 20, 2025, https://player.fm/series/masters-of-scale-1425703/how-to-raise-172m-for-the-underinvested-with-stacy-brown-philpot.

9 Paula Davis, "Building Your Resilience—the Skills You Need," Stress & Resilience Institute, 2025, https://stressandresilience.com/building-your-resilience-the-skills-you-need.

10 Whitney Johnson, *Disrupt Yourself: Master Relentless Change and Speed Up Your Learning Curve* (Harvard Business Review Press, 2019).

11 Johnson, *Disrupt Yourself.*

12 Susan MacKenty Brady, *Mastering Your Inner Critic and 7 Other High Hurdles to Advancement: How the Best Women Leaders Practice Self-Awareness to Change What Really Matters* (McGraw-Hill, 2018).

Chapter 3

1 Salesforce, "New Salesforce Data Reveals Top Drivers of Exceptional Employee Experience. Spoiler Alert: It's Not Free Snacks," Salesforce.com, September 15, 2022, www.salesforce.com/news/stories/how-to-engage-employees-2022.

2 Kim Clark, Jonathan Clark, and Erin Clark, "How Leaders Can Earn Power from Their People—Instead of Demanding It," Next Big Idea Club, September 18, 2024, https://nextbigideaclub.com/magazine/leaders-can-earn-power-people-instead-demanding-bookbite/51751.

3 Deloitte Insights, "Becoming Irresistible: A New Model for Employee Engagement," *Deloitte Review*, January 27, 2015, www.deloitte.com/us/en/insights/topics/talent/employee-engagement-strategies.html.

4 Joe Kittel, "Return-on-Investment for Spirituality," SPiBR.org LLC, 2023, https://spibr.org/roi-for-spirituality.

5 Deloitte, "Purpose Is Everything," Intelligent Enterprise Institute, July 19, 2023, https://medium.com/intelligent-enterprise-institute/purpose-is-everything-6cd275567a82.

6 The Universal House of Justice, "Letter to the Bahá'ís of the World About Economic Life," the Bahá'í International Community, March 1, 2017, https://universalhouseofjustice.bahai.org/involvement-life-society/20170301_001.

7 The Universal House of Justice, "Letter to the Bahá'ís of the World About Economic Life."

8 Innisfree Hotels, "Our Culture," accessed September 26, 2025, https://innisfreecorp.com/culture.

9 Ben & Jerry's, "This Is Why Fossil Fuel Was Buried in the Flavor Graveyard," Ben & Jerry's Homemade, November 16, 2016, www.benjerry.com/whats-new/archive/2016/fossil-fuel-divestment.

10 Bahá'u'lláh, "Epistle to the Son of the Wolf," trans. Shoghi Effendi, the Bahá'í Faith, Bahá'í Reference Library, accessed September 26, 2025, www.bahai.org/library/authoritative-texts/bahaullah/epistle-son-wolf/3#485843968.

11 John Donne, "Meditation XVII," in *Devotions upon Emergent Occasions* (A.M. for Thomas Iones, 1624), 109.

12 The Universal House of Justice, "Letter to the Bahá'ís of the World About Economic Life."

13 Marc Benioff and Monica Langley, *Trailblazer: The Power of Business as the Greatest Platform for Change* (Crown Currency, 2019).

14 Staff Author, "PEOPLE's 100 Companies That Care in 2023: Employers Putting Their Communities First," *People*, July 11, 2024, https://people.com/human-interest-people-100-companies-that-care-7749999?utm_source.

15 Barbara McEvilley, Ashby Monk, and Jason Voss, "De-Biasing Investment Decisions: The Role of Mindfulness," Addepart Research Brief, 2023, https://longterminvesting.stanford.edu/sites/g/files/sbiybj23856/files/media/file/addepar-debiasing-investment-decisions.pdf.

16 Charlie Munger, "The Psychology of Human Misjudgment," JamesClear.com, accessed September 26, 2025, https://jamesclear.com/great-speeches/psychology-of-human-misjudgment-by-charlie-munger.

Chapter 4

1 Shoghi Effendi, "The World Order of Baha'u'llah," the Bahá'í Faith, Bahá'í Reference Library, accessed September 26, 2025, https://www.bahai.org/library/authoritative-texts/shoghi-effendi/world-order-bahaullah/1#369510938.

2 Resolution Foundation. *Efforts to Tackle Britain's Epidemic of Poor Mental Health Should Focus on Lower Qualified Young People*. Press release, November 27, 2023. https://www.resolutionfoundation.org/press-releases/efforts-to-tackle-britains-epidemic-of-poor-mental-health-should-focus-on-lower-qualified-young-people/.

3 Sally Percy, "How Leaders Can Instill Hope in Their Teams," *Forbes*, March 5, 2024, www.forbes.com/sites/sallypercy/2024/03/05/how-leaders-can-instill-hope-in-their-teams.

4 Employee engagement refers to the emotional commitment and enthusiasm employees have toward their work and organization, driving them to contribute their best effort and stay motivated.

5 Jim Harter, "US Employee Engagement Sinks to 10-Year Low," Gallup, January 13, 2025, https://www.gallup.com/workplace/654911/employee-engagement-sinks-year-low.aspx.

6 meQuilibrium. *Don't Underestimate the Remarkable Power of Hope in the Workplace, New meQ Survey Says.* Accessed December 5, 2025. https://www.mequilibrium.com/resources/dont-underestimate-the-remarkable-power-of-hope-in-the-workplace-new-meq-survey-says/.

7 Harter, "US Employee Engagement Sinks to 10-Year Low."

8 'Abdu'l-Bahá in America, "Public Talks of 'Abdu'l-Bahá: For You I Desire Spiritual Distinction," June 15, 1912, https://centenary.bahai.us/talk/you-i-desire-spiritual-distinction.

9 Dylan Taylor, "Active Listening and Empathy for Better Working Relationships," *Forbes*, July 28, 2023, www.forbes.com/councils/forbesbusinesscouncil/2023/07/28/active-listening-and-empathy-for-better-working-relationships.

10 Hillel International, "'If I Am Not for Myself, Who Will Be for Me?' A Discussion for Developing a Practice of Self-Care," February 28, 2021, www.hillel.org/if-i-am-not-for-myself-who-will-be-for-me-a-discussion-for-developing-a-practice-of-self-care.

11 Brené Brown, *The Gifts of Imperfection: Let Go of Who You Think You're Supposed to Be and Embrace Who You Are* (Hazelden, 2010).

12 Brené Brown, "All Activity," LinkedIn, November 8, 2024, www.linkedin.com/in/brenebrown/recent-activity/all.

13 US Department of Justice, Office of Justice Programs, "Hope Research Center: 2024 Building Knowledge Through Research Award," accessed September 26, 2025, https://ovc.ojp.gov/gallery/award-recipients/2024/hope-research-center.

14 Princeton University, Office of Religious Life, "The Healing Power of Hope," accessed September 26, 2025, https://religiouslife.princeton.edu/worship-events/healing-power-hope?utm_source.com.

15 Jennifer Aaker, Melani Rudd, and Kathleen Vohs, "Awe Expands People's Perception of Time, Alters Decision Making, and Enhances Well-Being," Working Paper No. 2095, Stanford Graduate School of Business, 2012, www.gsb.stanford.edu/faculty-research/working-papers/awe-expands-peoples-perception-time-alters-decision-making-enhances.

16 Eric Barker, "Interview—Stanford Professor Jennifer Aaker on How to Increase Happiness and Meaning in Life," Barking Up the Wrong Tree, February 2013, https://bakadesuyo.com/2013/02/happiness-aaker-meaning-interview.

17 Jane Goodall and Douglas Abrams with Gail Hudson, *The Book of Hope: A Survival Guide for Trying Times* (Celadon Books, 2021).

Chapter 5

1 Attributed to 'Abdu'l-Bahá, *'Abdu'l-Bahá on Divine Philosophy*, comp. Isabel Fraser Chamberlain (Tudor Press, 1918), 115.

2 The Universal House of Justice, "The Promise of World Peace," the Bahá'í International Community, October 1985, https://www.bahai.org/library/authoritative-texts/the-universal-house-of-justice/messages/19851001_001/19851001_001.pdf.

3 Board of Governors of the Federal Reserve System, "DFA: Distributional Financial Accounts," last updated September 19, 2025, www.federalreserve.gov/releases/z1/dataviz/dfa/distribute/chart.

4 Jamey Keaten, "Billionaires' Wealth Soared in 2024, Anti-Poverty Group Says as the Elites Prepare for Another Davos," AP News, January 20, 2025, https://apnews.com/article/davos-2025-trump-wef-elon-musk-billionaires-ee121c56f6828021cb864de927383c7b.

5 Shoghi Effendi, "The World Order of Baha'u'llah."

6 The Universal House of Justice, "Letter to an Individual," the Bahá'í International Community, May 13, 1996, https://bahai-library.com/uhj_disintegration_world_order.

7 Patagonia, "Environmental and Social Footprint," accessed September 29, 2025, www.patagonia.com/our-footprint.

8 See https://unglobalcompact.org.

9 Universal House of Justice, "Letter to All National Spiritual Assemblies," The Bahá'í International Community, November 26, 2012, www.bahai.org/library/authoritative-texts/the-universal-house-of-justice/messages/20121126_001/1#151895117.

10 Ben & Jerry's, "Our Values, Activism and Mission," Ben & Jerry's Homemade, accessed September 29, 2025, www.benjerry.com/values.

11 B Lab, "B Impact Assessment," accessed September 29, 2025, www.bcorporation.net/en-us/programs-and-tools/b-impact-assessment.

12 Universal House of Justice, "Letter to All National Spiritual Assemblies."

13 See https://acumen.org/what-we-do.

14 See https://rootcapital.org.

15 Universal House of Justice, "Letter to All National Spiritual Assemblies."

16 Salesforce, "Philanthropy," accessed September 29, 2025, www.salesforce.com/company/philanthropy/?utm_source.com.

17 Ranjay Gulati, *Deep Purpose: The Heart and Soul of High-Performance Companies* (Harper Business, 2022), xvii.

18 Gulati, *Deep Purpose.*

19 See https://www.synergos.org/our-work/spiritual-civilization.

20 Judd Allen, *Better Together: How to Support the Proactive Mental Health of Family, Friends, and Coworkers* (Human Resources Institute, 2023).

21 Mental Health America, "Quick Facts and Statistics About Mental Health," accessed September 29, 2025, https://mhanational.org/resources/quick-facts-and-statistics-about-mental-health.

Chapter 6

1 'Abdu'l-Bahá, *'Abdu'l-Bahá in London* (Bahá'í Publishing Trust, 1982), 91.

2 Bahá'u'lláh, *Tabernacle of Unity* (Bahá'í World Center, 2006).

3 Lyazzat Yangaliyeva and Timur Chekparbayev, hosts, *In Conversation*, podcast, "Podcast Explores Contributions to Prevalent Discourses in Kazakhstan," February 3, 2025, https://news.bahai.org/story/1780.

4 The Bahá'í International Community, "Bahá'í International Community's Oral Statement to the 50th Session of the Commission for Social Development," February 2, 2012, www.bic.org/videos/elimination-extremes-poverty-and-wealth.

5 The Universal House of Justice, "Five-Year Plan Message 2016–2021," the Bahá'í International Community, December 29, 2015, www.bahai.org/library/authoritative-texts/the-universal-house-of-justice/messages/20151229_001/1#275100978.

6 Anuja Vaidya, "States Ranked by Percentage of Diabetics," Becker's Hospital Review, March 6, 2020, www.beckershospitalreview.com/rankings-and-ratings/states-ranked-by-percentage-of-diabetics/?utm_source=chatgpt.com.

7 Yajun Zhang, Fangfang Zhou, and Jianghau Mao, "Ethical Leadership and Follower Moral Actions: Investigating an Emotional Linkage," *Frontiers in Psychology* 4, no. 9 (2018), https://pmc.ncbi.nlm.nih.gov/articles/PMC6180164.

8 Mehran C. Ferdowsian, "Change Your Culture by Developing Core Competencies," Strategic Competencies, 2024, https://strategiccompetencies.com/competencies-developed.

9 Yuliya Chernova, "Ulu Ventures Raises $208 Million for Fourth Fund Amid DEI Backlash," *Wall Street Journal*, February 12, 2025, www.wsj.com/articles/ulu-ventures-raises-208-million-for-fourth-fund-amid-dei-backlash-717c7fe2.

10 The Bahá'í Faith, Bahá'í Reference Library, "Tablets of Bahá'u'lláh," the Bahá'í International Community, 2025, www.bahai.org/library/authoritative-texts/bahaullah/tablets-bahaullah.

11 Martin Luther King Jr., "Remaining Awake Through a Great Revolution: Commencement Address for Oberlin College," Oberlin College, June 1965, www2.oberlin.edu/external/EOG/BlackHistoryMonth/MLK/CommAddress.html.

12 Martin Luther King, Jr., Detroit, Michigan, February 28, 1954.

13 Deborah Perry Piscione and Josh Drean, "How Emerging Technologies Can Foster Human Connections at Work," *Harvard Business Review*, January 28, 2025, https://hbr.org/2025/01/how-emerging-technologies-can-foster-human-connections-at-work.

14 Piscione and Drean, "How Emerging Technologies Can Foster Human Connections at Work."

15 Ethical Business Building the Future, "How Emerging Technologies Can Foster Human Connections at Work: A Values-Driven Perspective," LinkedIn, February 2025, www.linkedin.com/posts/ebbf-mindful-people-meaningful-work_humannobility-justice-humanconnection-activity-7290088416946335745-2gFA?utm_source=share&utm_medium=member_desktop&rcm=ACoAAAZkPZUBujJpL57BICJSaEy4HmncU-UBc8-k.

16 Alex Shashkevich, "Virtual Reality Can Help Make People More Compassionate Compared to Other Media, New Stanford Study Finds," Stanford Report, October 17, 2018, https://news.stanford.edu/stories/2018/10/virtual-reality-can-help-make-people-empathetic.

17 The Universal House of Justice, "Letter to All National Spiritual Assemblies."

18 ÆRTH, "Planetary Intelligence," accessed September 29, 2025, www.aerth.live.

19 Adina Popescu and Carl Hayden-Smith, "New ÆRTH Rising," Apiary Studios, October 2021, https://apiarystudios.org/antenna/zine-new-aerth-rising.

20 In finance, alpha is a measure of an investment's performance that indicates the excess return it generates above a benchmark or market index, adjusted for the level of risk taken.

21 Soul.com, "Soul-Driven Leadership," accessed September 29, 2025, www.soul.com/soul-driven-leadership.

Chapter 7

1 Hrund Gunnsteinsdottir, *Innsaei: Heal, Revive, and Reset with the Icelandic Art of Intuition* (HarperOne, 2025).

Conclusion

1 Lynne Twist, *The Soul of Money: Transforming Your Relationship with Money and Life* (W. W. Norton, 2017).

ABOUT THE AUTHOR

Jenna Nicholas is an investor, entrepreneur, and author. She is an active member of the Bahá'í Faith and passionate about inspiring readers to invest with purpose. As president of Light-Post Capital, an investment and acquisition firm, and CEO of Impact Experience, she has led initiatives that bridge climate, health care, education, and investing for social good. Nicholas's work as an angel investor has supported innovative ventures, and she has championed global coalitions, shifting billions of dollars toward sustainable solutions. Her experience spans roles at the World Bank Treasury and Calvert Special Equities, and she has shared her journey on the TEDx stage. She has been recognized as a Forbes 30 Under 30 Social Entrepreneur, a Council on Foreign Relations member, a PD Soros fellow, a Stanford Social Innovation fellow, and an Echoing Green fellow, and holds BA and MBA degrees from Stanford, in addition to having studied at Oxford. Nicholas lived in Beijing for several years, where she taught at Tsinghua University School of Economics and Management. She has been featured in the *New York Times*, *Financial Times*, and *Forbes*, among other publications.